Contents

Introduction
Law and Gospel:
   The Hallmark of Classical Lutheranism   5
      Rev. Dr. Carl E. Braaten

A Reformed Account
   of the Law-Gospel Distinction   19
      Rev. Dr. Michael S. Horton

Law and Gospel:
   Separators, Confusers, and Preachers   49
      Rev. Dr. Steven D. Paulson

Law and Gospel since Vatican II   55
   Rev. Dr. Jared Wicks, S. J.

Did Luther Get Paul Right on Justification?   67
   Dr. Stephen Westerholm

Law, Gospel, and the Beloved Community   91
   Rev. Dr. Paul R. Hinlicky

The Third Use of the Law:
   Freedom and Obedience in the Christian Life   115
      Rev. Dr. Piotr J. Malysz

A Resurrection Hermeneutic:
   Law and Gospel in Preaching and Worship   141
      Rev. Dr. Amy C. Schifrin

Preaching Law and Gospel   163
   Rev. Dr. J. Larry Yoder

Presenters

Rev. Dr. Carl E. Braaten
    Professor Emeritus of Systematic Theology
    Lutheran School of Theology at Chicago
    Sun City West, Arizona

Rev. Dr. Paul R. Hinlicky
    Tise Professor of Lutheran Studies at Roanoke College
    Salem, Virginia

Rev. Dr. Michael S. Horton
    Professor of Theology and Apologetics
    Westminster Seminary California
    Escondido, California

Rev. Dr. Piotr J. Malysz
    Assistant Professor of Theology
    Beeson Divinity School
    Birmingham, Alabama

Rev. Dr. Steven D. Paulson
    Professor of Systematic Theology
    Luther Seminary
    St. Paul, Minnesota

Rev. Dr. Amy C. Schifrin
    Pastor, Mission in Christ and Faith Lutheran Churches
    Strawberry Point, Iowa

Dr. Stephen Westerholm
    Associate Professor of Biblical Studies
    McMaster University
    Hamilton, Ontario, Canada

Rev. Dr. Jared Wicks, S. J.
    Resident Scholar, Pontifical College Josephinum
    Columbus, Ohio

Rev. Dr. J. Larry Yoder
    Professor of Religion
    Lenoir-Rhyne University
    Hickory, North Carolina

Preaching and Teaching
the Law and Gospel of God

CONTRIBUTORS
Carl E. Braaten
Paul R. Hinlicky
Michael S. Horton
Piotr J. Malysz
Steven D. Paulson
Amy C. Schifrin
Stephen Westerholm
Jared Wicks, S. J.
J. Larry Yoder

Edited with an Introduction by
Carl E. Braaten

Papers Delivered at a Theological Conference
Sponsored by Lutheran CORE
and the
North American Lutheran Church
August 15-16, 2012

Calvary Lutheran Church, Golden Valley, Minnesota

ALPB Books
Delhi, New York

For a FREE COPY of
Lutheran Forum and *Forum Letter*
go online at: www.lutheranforum.org
and click on "Free Issue"

Cover photo of the steeple of
Calvary Lutheran Church, Golden Valley, Minnesota,
by Frederick J. Schumacher

The American Lutheran Publicity Bureau wishes to acknowledge with deep appreciation the work of William Fensterer in proofreading of the text, Dorothy A. Zelenko for assistance with photo artwork, and Martin A. Christiansen for layout and design work.

Frederick J. Schumacher
Executive Director, ALPB

2013 © ALPB Books
All rights reserved in the United States of America

ISBN 1-892921-23-5

American Lutheran Publicity Bureau
PO Box 327
Delhi, NY 13753

Preaching and Teaching the Law and Gospel of God
(Delhi, NY: ALPB Books, 2013), 174 pp.

Introduction
Law and Gospel:
The Hallmark of Classical Lutheranism

Carl E. Braaten

The theme of this theological conference is "preaching and teaching the law and gospel of God." The wording is important. It says that we are dealing not so much with a classical doctrine for theologians to retrieve and debate. Rather, our theme is about what preachers are called and ordained to do, week after week – to proclaim the gospel of salvation in such a way as not to confuse it with the law. For the covenant people of God, starting with Abraham and his descendants, the promise of God preceded the giving of the law to Moses on Mount Sinai. The law was given not as a way to salvation but as a way of ordering life in obedience to God. No individual and no society can flourish without giving the law its due. If as preachers and teachers we learn to make the proper distinction between law and gospel, we need not worry so much about the state of the church. For such preaching holds the key to the renewal and reform of the church in every age. *Ecclesia semper reformanda!* The church is always in need of reform and renewal, but that will not happen, it cannot happen, unless the preaching and teaching going on in the churches is such as to "rightly divide the Word of truth" (II Timothy 2: 15).

But, of course, the law/gospel distinction is not a doctrine unto itself. Rather, it is the essential corollary of the Pauline-Augustinian-Reformation article of justification by faith apart from the works of the law. Martin Luther made it clear that the two go together; we cannot get either one right without the other. If we listen to the words of the prophet Isaiah, we will "look to the rock from which we were hewn" (Isaiah 51: 1) and that's what this conference is all about.

From Martin Luther to Philip Melanchthon, from John Gerhard to Gerhard Forde, from C. F. W. Walther to Werner Elert – these theologians, not always in agreement among themselves, did their best to make clear that the Scriptures inculcate the twofold Word of God, both law and gospel, and as such they are not to be equated or confused. These teachers span nearly 500 years in which Lutheranism has confessed to the wider Christian world that the main purpose of rightly distinguishing law and gospel is to lift high the cross of Jesus Christ for the salvation of the world.

Fifty years ago, October 11, 1962, to be precise, Pope John XXIII opened the Second Vatican Council. That inaugurated the ecumenical era in which Lutherans and virtually all major church bodies have engaged in multiple dialogues about what unites and divides them.

Lutherans have affirmed in these dialogues that the law-gospel principle exists both for the sake of interpreting the Bible aright – hermeneutics – and for the sake of preaching the whole counsel of God – homiletics. So, the question naturally pops up: is this law/gospel principle alien to all the other traditions? Do they also apply it, and if so, do they do so in the same way? Do we find an awareness of this distinction between law and gospel in the Roman Catholic tradition? Do we find it among churches in the Calvinist Reformed tradition? Do we find it being observed by Anglican and Orthodox theologians?

Walter Kasper, former president of the Pontifical Council for Promoting Christian Unity, a veteran ecumenist and one of the best, regards it as regrettable that "law and gospel" never became a major theme in Catholic theology.[1] The *Catechism of the Catholic Church* has much to say about the law of all kinds, but nothing that resembles the Lutheran paradigm of law and gospel. Avery Dulles found traces of the law-gospel contrast in

---

1. Walter Kasper, "Law and Gospel," *Sacramentum Mundi* (New York: Herder and Herder, 1969), 3:297.

pre-Reformation tradition, certainly in Augustine and Aquinas, but then he admits: "It was not thematically taken up by Trent, nor has it been in modern Catholic systematics."[2]

The *Joint Declaration on the Doctrine of Justification* does contain a section on "Law and Gospel."[3] There it states: "We confess together (Lutherans and Catholics) that persons are justified by faith in the gospel 'apart from the works prescribed by the law' (Rom. 3: 28). Christ has fulfilled the law and by his death and resurrection has overcome it as a way to salvation."

The matter is quite different with the Reformed tradition. In his *Institutes of the Christian Religion*, John Calvin taught as emphatically as Luther that the Word of God contains two parts: the one is the law and the other is the gospel. There is gospel in the Old Testament and there is law in the New Testament. Lutherans and Calvinists have been in agreement on that. Yet, they have had disagreements in centuries past on the usefulness of the law in the Christian life. In *Marburg Revisited*, a candid statement approved by Lutheran and Reformed theologians in the 1960s, longstanding differences between their respective traditions were acknowledged. They stated: "We are agreed both that Jesus Christ is the fulfillment and end of the law, and that in the Christian life God continues to lay his claim upon the redeemed; but we are not agreed how to denominate that claim, whether law or gospel. Both Calvinists and Lutherans know themselves to be saved through the gospel and called to Christian obedience."[4] But it became clear that for these dialogue partners such differences no longer should make much difference, at least not a difference so great as to keep the churches divided. That began the process which eventually culminated in full communion agreements between a few Lutheran and

---

2. Avery Dulles, S. J., "Justification in Contemporary Catholic Theology," *Justification by Faith, Lutherans and Catholics in Dialogue* VII, Edited by H. George Anderson, T. Austin Murphy, and Joseph A. Burgess (Minneapolis: Augsburg Publishing House, 1985), p. 276.

3. *Joint Declaration on the Doctrine of Justification*, 1997, Law and Gospel, 4.5. 31-33.

4. *Marburg Revisited, A Reexamination of Lutheran and Reformed Traditions*, edited by Paul C. Empie and James I. McCord (Minneapolis: Augsburg Publishing House, 1966), p. 152.

Reformed churches. Some Lutherans are happy with the outcome, some are not.

We are fortunate to have three experts to take us into the thick of the law/gospel debate, involving Lutheran, Reformed, and Roman Catholic traditions – the Rev. Dr. Michael S. Horton, the Rev. Dr. Steven D. Paulson, and the Rev. Dr. Jared Wicks, Society of Jesus.

They will be given a proper introduction shortly.

The Doctrine of Justification

C. F. W. Walther is generally considered the greatest theologian in the history of the Lutheran Church–Missouri Synod. He said something that most Lutherans would agree to: "Now, of all doctrines the most important is the doctrine of justification. However, immediately following upon it, as second in importance, is this, how Law and Gospel are to be divided."[5] We might have reason to quibble with these generalizations. Luther did not always have justification on his brain. He wrote the *Small Catechism* and the *Large Catechism* to teach the essentials of the Christian faith, but he did not use the word "justification" even once. Moreover, neither the teaching on law and gospel nor the doctrine of justification can be abstracted from the entire biblical meta-narrative from the alpha of creation to the omega of redemption. Paul's teaching on justification is important and true, but it is not the whole enchilada. My favorite gospel, the Gospel of John, never refers to justification or any of its cognate terms. Nevertheless, in dealing with law and gospel we must take up the doctrine of justification, because just as it addressed the crisis in the church of the 16th century, so also it may give us the appropriate word for the crisis in which we find ourselves at this point in church history.

We still today affirm our traditional Lutheran teaching that God justifies the ungodly for Christ's sake through faith apart from the works of the law. Our Confession states: "Nothing in

---

5. C. F. W. Walther, *The Proper Distinction Between Law and Gospel* (St. Louis: Concordia Publishing House, 1928), p. 5.

this article can be given up or compromised.... On this article rests all that we teach."[6] But is it not something of a shame that we Lutherans have squabbled so much over what it truly means? Schisms have occurred because of our lack of consensus. For example, the difference between confessional orthodox and evangelical pietist Lutherans on justification is like night and day. The orthodox party accuses the pietists of semi-Pelagianism. What's the problem?

Can't we just all get along? Imagine the difficulty Lutherans must have had in reaching an agreement with Roman Catholics in their "Joint Declaration on the Doctrine of Justification" when we cannot even agree among ourselves. When I attended Luther Seminary in the 1950s, this was the chief point of contention between two factions on the faculty, one led by Herman Preus and the other by George Aus. And, of course, students took sides, and some switched from one side to the other.

The Lutheran Confessors oppose the idea that good works contribute to salvation. But if justification is BY faith, what if faith itself is smuggled back in as a good work that sinners must somehow do to be justified? What if faith is conceived of as an instrumental or meritorious *cause* of justification, in the sense that justification occurs *because* of faith? To be sure, faith is a good work, but it is the good work of God. It's the work of the Holy Spirit. Faith does say, "I believe," but the fact that I believe is not due to my ability, my decision, or an exercise of my free will – because my will is not free to so believe.

Luther's explanation of the Third Article of the Apostles' Creed makes clear what every Lutheran confirmand used to learn by heart. "I believe that I cannot by my own reason or strength believe in Jesus Christ my Lord, or come to him. But the Holy Spirit has called me through the Gospel, enlightened me with his gifts, and sanctified and kept me in the true faith." Many Lutherans became so frightened by the doctrine of predestination that, contrary to Luther, they adopted the semi-Pelagian concept of free will, along with Erasmus of Rotterdam.

---

6. Smalcald Articles, *Book of Concord*, Tappert Edition, p. 292, II, 1.

The evangelical pietists abandoned Luther's teaching in *The Bondage of the Will*. Luther said this was his best book; you can get rid of all the rest.[7] The question is simply this: Is God the source and power not only of justification but also of the faith that clings to Christ? Is faith itself the gift of God or are we fallen sinners free to turn it on or off, like cold or hot running water? Having been kicked out of Eden, are we free to return to paradise on our own choosing? Genuine Lutheran teaching holds that our will is bound by sin and Satan and that faith is not a work that lies within the grasp of human possibility. Many fear that such a view denies human freedom, but in truth it places freedom where it really belongs, in the hands of a gracious and omnipotent God.

Muddled thinking about justification was embarrassingly highlighted in 1963 when Lutheran delegates from around the world gathered in Helsinki for an assembly of the Lutheran World Federation. They met there to draft a new statement on justification by faith in language that modern people would understand. After ten days of discussion, debate, and disagreement, they offered this excuse for failing to produce a statement: "The man of today no longer asks (Luther's question), 'How can I find a gracious God?' He suffers not from God's wrath, but from the impression of his absence, not from sin, but from the meaninglessness of his own existence; he asks not about a gracious God, but whether God really exists."[8] Before making such a suicidal concession, they should have read something Karl Barth wrote ten years before: "Of all the superficial catchwords of our age, surely one of the most superficial is that, whereas 16th century man was occupied with the grace of God, modern man is much more radically concerned about God

---

7. Luther wrote this in a letter to Wolfgang Capito, July 9, 1537. "Regarding the plan to collect my writings in volumes, I am quite cool and not at all eager about it because, roused by a Saturnian hunger, I would rather see them all devoured. For I acknowledge none of them to be a book of mine, except the one. 'On the Bound Will' and the Catechism."

8. *Proceedings of the Fourth Assembly of the LWF*, 1963 (Berlin: Lutherisches Verlagshaus, 1965), 57ff.

himself and as such."[9] I have called this Lutheran assembly the Helsinki fiasco.[10]

Adding to this confusion internal to Lutheran theology is the attack on the Reformation doctrine of justification by some contemporary biblical scholars, most notably E. P. Sanders, James Dunn, and N. T. Wright. Luther expounded Paul's teaching of the righteousness of God in Galatians and Romans. But what if Luther misinterpreted Paul, as these scholars claim he did? What if they are right that Luther was wrong about Paul's argument with Judaism? What if Luther was guilty of reading Paul through the lens of his personal struggles and his polemic against the alleged legalism of his Roman Catholic opponents? Dr. Stephen Westerholm is an expert on the theology of the apostle Paul. He will address our conference on the topic: "Did Luther Get Paul Right on the Doctrine of Justification?"

What Does the Law-Gospel Paradigm Have to Do with the Church?

The purpose of the church is to preach the gospel of salvation in the name of the triune God to all the nations until the end of time. Sinners are justified by grace through faith and become members of Christ's church in baptism. Lutherans and Catholics in dialogue worked for decades to remove the mutual condemnations of the sixteenth century and to reach an agreement on the doctrine of justification. Still the two Communions are divided. What stands between them? This question is still on the table.

Lutherans need to get their own act together to better understand the linkage between justification by faith and the nature of the church. What does the distinction between law and gospel have to do with ecclesiology, the church and its mission, its nature and purpose? We believe in the justifying word of the gospel and we believe in the one holy catholic church. These two articles of faith must be interconnected, because the sav-

---

9. Karl Barth, *Church Dogmatics*, IV/1, p.530.
10. Carl E. Braaten, *Justification: The Article by Which the Church Stands or Falls* (Minneapolis: Fortress Press, 1990).

ing work of God in Jesus Christ is the church's one and only foundation. It is not satisfactory to say that Lutherans are strong on soteriology, the doctrine of salvation, but weak on ecclesiology, the doctrine of the church. That may be historically true, but it is not theologically acceptable in an ecumenical age. We have invited a theologian well known to all of us to speak on this topic: the Rev. Dr. Paul R. Hinlicky.

Controversy on the Third Use of the Law

When embroiled in a family quarrel it is necessary to go back to better move forward. So let us look to the rock from which we were hewn. Martin Luther said this: "Whoever knows well how to distinguish the gospel from the law should give thanks to God and know that he is a real theologian."[11] "Place any person who is well versed in this art of dividing the law from the gospel at the head and call him a doctor of Holy Writ."[12] Well, we have a lot of theologians with doctorates who would flunk the test. More of Luther: "The knowledge of this topic, this distinction between the law and the gospel, is necessary to the highest degree; for it contains a summary of all Christian doctrine."[13] "We must know what the law is, and what the gospel is. The law commands and requires us to do certain things. The law is directed solely to our behavior and consists in making requirements. For God speaks through the law, saying, 'Do this, avoid that, this is what I expect of you.' The gospel, however, does not preach what we are to do or to avoid. It sets up no requirements, but reverses the approach of the law, does the very opposite, and says, 'This is what God has done for you; for he has let his Son be made flesh for you, has let him be put to death for your sake....' For the gospel teaches exclusively what has been given us by God, and not – as in the case of the law – what we are to do and give to God."[14]

---

11. LW, 26, p. 115.

12. Scott R. Murray, *Law, Life, and the Living God* (St. Louis: Concordia Publishing House, 2002), p. 16.

13. LW, 26, p. 117.

14. LW, 35, p. 162.

It has become fashionable for some Luther scholars to drive a wedge between Luther and Melanchthon. Melanchthon was known to do some flip-flopping on the doctrine of the law, but as John Witte has shown in his magisterial work on the law in the Lutheran Reformation,[15] for the most part Melanchthon stood with Luther on distinguishing law and gospel. This is what Melanchthon wrote: "There are two chief works of God in men, to terrify and to justify.... One or the other of these works is spoken of throughout Scripture. One part is the law, which reveals, denounces, and condemns sin. The other part is the gospel, that is, the promise of grace granted in Christ."[16]

But not everything was going so swimmingly among Luther's friends and followers. John Agricola was a friend of Luther. But he was suspicious of Melanchthon for teaching that the law continues to apply to Christians after their conversion. For Agricola this was tantamount to a betrayal of the gospel. The gospel and not the law, he said, is to be preached in the church. He famously said, "Good works are injurious to salvation." That set ablaze the antinomian controversy. To the opposite side, George Major, a friend of Melanchthon, feared that this would open the flood gates to wanton licentiousness among Christians. He taught that good works are necessary to salvation.

Ever since then the pendulum has been swinging back and forth, either to the side of legalism, where the pressure of the law overcomes gospel freedom, or to the side of antinomianism, where ignoring the law leads to moral laxity. Good works have suffered an ambiguous fate in Lutheran preaching. Professor Paul Holmer of Yale Divinity School chided Lutheran preachers for slamming good works as though the doing of them has been one of the great temptations facing Lutheran folks. The Confessions are clear: good works are not necessary as a way of salvation, but Christians are called to do good works anyway, whether driven by love or conscience, because our neighbor needs them.

---

15. John Witte, Jr., *Law and Protestantism: The Legal Teachings of the Lutheran Reformation* (Cambridge University Press, 2002).

16. Apology of the Augsburg Confession, Article XII, *Book of Concord*, Tappert Edition, p. 189.

The *Formula of Concord* tried to end the discord among the first generation of Lutherans. Article V formulates the Lutheran teaching of law and gospel about which there was substantial consensus. It states: "The distinction between law and gospel is an especially brilliant light which serves the purpose that the Word of God may be rightly divided and the writings of the holy prophets and apostles may be explained and understood correctly. We must therefore observe this distinction with particular diligence lest we confuse the two doctrines and change the gospel into law.... For this reason and in order that both doctrines, law and gospel, may not be mingled together and confused so that what belongs to one doctrine is ascribed to the other, it is necessary to urge and to maintain with all diligence the true and proper distinction between law and gospel, and diligently to avoid anything that might give occasion for a confusion between them by which the two doctrines would be tangled together and made into one doctrine.... Strictly speaking, the gospel is the promise of forgiveness of sins and justification through Christ, whereas the law is a message that rebukes and condemns sin."[17]

There we have the gist of our confessional teaching on law and gospel and their proper distinction. I am calling it the hallmark of classical Lutheranism. However, the happy consensus that Article V of the *Formula of Concord* has enjoyed ends in the case of Article VI, that deals with "The Third Use of the Law." This has to do with the role of the law in the Christian life. This is without doubt the most controversial topic in Lutheran dogmatics from the 16th to the 21st centuries. It tries to navigate between the Scylla of legalism and the Charybdis of antinomianism. As with most formulations of church doctrine that aim to straddle the divide between opposing parties, it is a compromise statement, no different in that respect from the Creeds of Nicaea and Chalcedon. It did not end the bickering, and the dispute concerning the third use of the law continues until to-

---

17. Solid Declaration, Article V, Law an Gospel, *Book of Concord*, Tappert Edition, pp. 558-563.

day.[18] We have invited Dr. Piotr Malysz to address the thorny issue of the third use of the law, giving due consideration to both the freedom of the gospel in Christ and obedience to the commandments of God in the Christian life.

Law and Gospel in Congregational Life

When we as Christians come together every Lord's Day, two things are supposed to happen – our reception of the Word of God in sermon and sacrament and our response in prayer, praise, and thanksgiving. The distinction between law and gospel is most important where the rubber hits the road in preaching and worship. As we said at the beginning, this distinction between law and gospel is not primarily something for theologians to discuss and debate. Rather, faithful preaching of the Word of God depends on the proper distinction between law and gospel. The abysmal state of preaching in the churches today may be due at least in part to confusion about what the gospel is and how it relates to the law.

The teaching of homiletics in our Lutheran seminaries has largely abandoned the law/gospel approach. Instead we've been told that preaching is story-telling, bringing your story to rhyme with God's story – with a lot of funny stories thrown in. The electronic media have encouraged the idea that preaching ought to be a form of entertainment. One Lutheran preacher has written about "entertainment evangelism." I can imagine that John Tetzel was at least entertaining. People flocked to hear him preach "cheap grace." "When the coin in the coffer rings; the soul from purgatory springs." People bought what he had to sell at a good discount. On most Sundays I sit in the pew, and at my age that adds up to a lot of Sundays. I've been asking myself whether preaching has really improved with the nearly total abandonment of the distinction between law and gospel. Certain biblical words have been largely deleted from pulpit use

---

18. Cf. Scott R. Murray, *Law, Life, and the Living God. The Third Use of the Law in Modern American Lutheranism* (St. Louis: Concordia Publishing House, 2002). Also, Edward A. Engelbrecht, *Friends of the Law. Luther's Use of the Law for the Christian Life* (St. Louis: Concordia Publishing House, 2011).

– words like sin, guilt, Satan, wrath, repentance, judgment, damnation, hell. And so the preaching of the law has come to a stop. It is too negative, turns people off; it's not entertaining.

But are we faring any better with the preaching of the gospel? When liberal Protestants call for the end of dogma, they lose all control of how to distinguish the biblical gospel from other varieties of religious expression. Without dogma your interpretation is as good as anyone else's, and there is no way to tell which is true. So even Lutheran preachers are known to mess with the proper name of the Triune God, Father, Son, and Holy Spirit, a name deeply etched into the primal dogma of biblical Nicene orthodoxy.

The distinction between law and gospel is a principle to guide those who choreograph the various steps, movements, and actions that take place when God's people enter a house of worship. If worship leaders do not adhere to this principle, they will inevitably be at the mercy of some other model, more in sync with the *Zeitgeist*. They may be driven by some kind of therapeutic psychology, political ideology, or gnostic spirituality. To help us think through the importance and relevance of the law/gospel distinction for preaching and worship today, we have invited two pastor-theologians to address this conference. They are the Rev. Dr. J. Larry Yoder and the Rev. Dr. Amy Schifrin.

Church Political Consequences

What theologians do has consequences for the policies and practices of the churches to which they belong. It is easy for theologians to be unaware of the effects of their teaching at the ground level. Often they are accused of living in an ivory tower, out of touch with the grassroots. The fact is, theology does matter, for good or ill. The troubles internal to the mainline Protestant denominations are due largely to a failure of theology. The ELCA's "Social Statement on Human Sexuality," for example, was written by a theologically challenged committee and passed by an assembly lacking sufficient theological discernment to withstand the seductions of current cultural values or the lack of them.

Theology makes a difference. With hindsight we now can see that the downhill slide of Lutheranism into antinomianism was prepared by what was being taught at the seminaries. Agape ethics, which at first sounded so Lutheran, turned out to be another term for situation ethics, the endorsement of moral relativism and the ethic of choice in campus ministry. Neglect and misinterpretation of the law-gospel paradigm led to unintended consequences.

Our generation of teachers – I include myself – failed the church, miserably. Too many of us abrogated our confessional teaching on law and gospel, and carried on as though Lutherans who love the "gospel" must at the same time be enemies of the law. Instead the seminaries became overloaded with copy cats mimicking the enticing isms and intoxicating slogans that came down the pike one after another. It was not the intention of most of the teachers of my generation to open the door to church policies that were cheered on by the acolytes of Hollywood. But we were impotent to stop it. Bishops and theologians and others in responsibility did not have the theological stuff to counter the ideology that was taking over the reins of leadership. There were some who saw the handwriting on the wall,[19] who like Daniel of old interpreted the meaning of "MENE , MENE, TEKEL, and PARSIN."[20] Which being interpreted states: "God has numbered the days of your kingdom and brought it to an end.... You have been weighed in the balance and found wanting.... Your kingdom is divided." Twenty five years later we are reaping what we sowed -- apostasy, heresy, and schism. The penitential Psalms take on new relevancy and potency. It may be a salutary thing for us to take some time for grieving, lamentation, and repentance, even as we press forward in hope, eager to discover what God still has in store for his church.

---

19. I have in mind the two "Call To Faithfulness Conferences" held at St. Olaf College in 1990 and 1992, sponsored by three Lutheran magazines: *Dialog – A Journal of Theology*, *Lutheran Quarterly*, and *Lutheran Forum*. All the addresses put the leadership of the ELCA on notice that they were taking the church in the wrong direction. The leaders either boycotted the meetings or turned a deaf ear.

20. Daniel 5, 25-26.

A Reformed Account of the Law-Gospel Distinction

Michael S. Horton

Reducing intellectual systems to a central dogma from which each principle is deduced and by which one could distinguish one from another was a reigning method among nineteenth-century historians. In view of such approaches in his day, B. B. Warfield complained, "It is unfortunate that a great body of the scientific discussion" throughout the nineteenth century "has been carried on somewhat vigorously with a view to determining the fundamental principle of Calvinism, has sought particularly to bring out its contrast with some other theological tendency, commonly with the sister Protestant tendency of Lutheranism." There are important differences. "But it is misleading to find the formative principle of either type of Protestantism in its difference from others." While Lutheranism and Reformed theology display unique characteristics, "They have infinitely more in common than in distinction. And certainly nothing could be more misleading than to represent them (as is often done) as owing their differences to their more pure embodiment respectively of the principle of predestination and that of justification by faith." Warfield added, "The doctrine of predestination is not the formative principle of Calvinism, the root from which it springs. It is one of its logical consequences, one of the branches which it has inevitably thrown out." If one is looking for a "central truth," Warfield explains, it is for Reformed theology's "complete dependence upon the free mercy of a saving God" and it is in defending this truth that predestination has its proper place. Nor is belief in predestination a Reformed peculiarity, but is simply "Augustinianism." "Just as little can the doctrine of justification by faith be represented as specifically Lutheran… Calvinism asks with Lutheranism, indeed, that most poignant of all questions, What shall I do to be saved? and answers it as Lutheranism answers it."

This zeal to distinguish the genius of Reformed theology can lead not only to the misrepresentation of other traditions, but to the disfigurement of historic Reformed theology itself.

Although the central dogma thesis has been discredited in recent scholarship, both in its method and conclusions, it continues to animate caricatures and reductionism. Following Barth's assimilation of the law to gospel, many of Barth's students (most notable Thomas and James Torrance) set Calvin against Reformed orthodoxy as if the latter were too "Lutheran" — or perhaps legalistic — in comparison with the Christocentrism of the great reformer. Charles Partee writes, "The main and specific point that Calvin makes in this section of the Institutes [Book 2] is that grace takes precedence over law." Collapsing these distinctions, however, Partee suggests that for Calvin "— the gracious law is God's promise of salvation and the gracious gospel is the fulfillment of that promise. In his earlier writings Calvin followed Luther's emphasis on and order of 'law before gospel,' but later, Calvin teaches that grace precedes law." Partee does not offer a footnote for this "later" view. Lacking such evidence, it seems more appropriate to accept that the diversity that Partee recognizes in Calvin on this point is due to the subtlety with which he uses the categories of law and gospel.

It is clear enough that Partee's main objection is to the developing Reformed tradition's correlation of law and gospel with the covenant of works and the covenant of grace, respectively. "The role of the law in the covenant of works is a post-Calvin topic." Again, this obscures more than it explains. Calvin certainly held that humanity "in Adam" is obligated to fulfill the law as a covenant of life and that Christ fulfilled this Adamic commission, meriting life for his posterity. In fact, the substance of the "covenant of law" is found in Irenaeus and Augustine. Ironically, given his strong statements of discontinuity above, Partee says, "Turning from the law's purpose to its effects, Calvin suggests that the moral law would produce eternal salvation if it could be completely observed (II.7.3). In this line Calvin veers closest to the Westminster Confession's concept of a once-valid-but-now-rejected covenant of works."

Closer to home — and with more nuance than some — Mark Garcia refers to Luther's "puzzling exhortation to believers" to ignore "the whole of active righteousness and the law," turning one's whole attention away from the law to grace. Yet he fails to mention precisely the same exhortation may be found in Calvin. In both cases, the question is how trembling questioners may find peace. Garcia follows Peter Lillback in contrasting Calvin's "covenantal" and Luther's "law-gospel" approach. Garcia judges, "Consequently, whereas Luther warned believers to avoid the law, Calvin pointed his readers to the biblical imperatives of covenantal obedience."

Although more recently the law-gospel distinction has been regarded by some as a Lutheran distinctive, it has been embraced in standard Reformed systems from Bullinger to Berkhof. As we will see, there are crucial differences in the way Lutheran and Reformed traditions developed this distinction. For example, the covenant theology that became part of the systematic architecture of Reformed interpretation introduced a more redemptive-historical treatment, over against the more abstract opposition of law and gospel in Lutheranism. Nevertheless, both traditions insisted upon the distinction as necessary for sound biblical interpretation, preaching, doctrine, and life.

The subject is large, so what follows is more of a summary of arguments than the arguments themselves. After a brief exegetical rationale, I will turn to the role that this distinction has played in Reformed theology.

An Exegetical Rationale for the Law-Gospel Distinction

As I explain below, the distinction between law and gospel was not only embraced in Reformed theology, but became the architectural structure of mature federalism. Above and before all historical covenants stands the eternal covenant of redemption, entered into by the persons of the Trinity. Establishing the unconditional basis of God's electing and redeeming purposes, this *pactum salutis* has as its goal the glory of God, exhibited supremely in the union of the elect with Christ in everlasting fellowship. The two major covenants with humanity are the covenant of creation (also called the covenant of works, nature, or law) and the covenant of grace. As the Westminster Confession summarizes,

> The first covenant made with man was a covenant of works, wherein life was promised to Adam; and in him to his posterity, upon condition of perfect and personal obedience. Man, by his fall, having made himself incapable of life by that covenant, the Lord was pleased to make a second, commonly called the covenant of grace; wherein he freely offereth unto sinners life and salvation by Jesus Christ; requiring of them faith in him, that they may be saved, and promising to give unto all those that are ordained to eternal life his Holy Spirit, to make them willing and able to believe.

Thus, these two covenants differ in their basis (fulfillment of the law rather than the inheritance promised in the gospel). They also are distinguished by the fact that Adam was the mediator of the first covenant, while Christ is the mediator of the second. Nevertheless, the covenant of works foreshadows Christ and the goal of both covenants is confirmation in everlasting blessedness. The blessings of the covenant of grace are a gift-inheritance to us because as the last Adam our Lord has fulfilled the covenant of works. Hence, "This covenant of grace is frequently set forth in Scripture by the name of a testament, in reference to the death of Jesus Christ the Testator, and to the everlasting inheritance, with all things belonging to it, therein bequeathed."

In my view, the best approach exegetically is to begin by comparing and contrasting the Abrahamic and Sinai covenants. To be sure, the relation between these covenants is more controversial in the history of Reformed interpretation than the relation between the covenant of works made with Adam and the covenant of grace promised after the fall. Nevertheless, it is in the relation between Sinai and Zion that Scripture most clearly impresses us with a clear distinction between law and gospel as different covenantal principles: namely, attainment and gift-inheritance. I have explored this exegetical territory at length elsewhere. Here I will only summarize the point by appealing to a few examples.

Challenging his opponents' conviction that salvation not only comes *from* the Jews but only comes to those who themselves *become* Jews, the Apostle to the Gentiles explains that there are two very different types of covenantal arrangements in the Old Testament itself. Paul speaks forcefully in Galatians 4 of two covenants, two mountains, and two mothers. There is a covenant of law established at Mount Sinai, engendering an earthly Jerusalem, which is identified with Hagar the slave, and a covenant of promise promised to Abraham and his seed, engendering a heavenly Jerusalem, which is identified with Sarah the free woman. Confusion of these two covenants, Paul believed, lay at the heart of the Galatian heresy, a charge repeated by the Protestant Reformers in the sixteenth century.

The principles of law (i.e., personal performance) and promise (i.e., inheritance of an estate by virtue of the performance of another) give rise to antithetical forms of religion. The inheritance, Paul insists, is either by our obedience to the law or by someone else's, bestowed on us by free grace alone; it cannot be by both. Being the beneficiary of an inheritance is not the same as being a successful partner who receives a reward for service rendered. Paul makes this point not only in Galatians, but in such places as Romans 3 and 4, where Abraham is once more presented as the paradigm case of justification through faith alone "apart from the deeds of the law," so that the inheritance (election, redemption, new life) may come to gentiles as well as Jews. Boasting is therefore entirely excluded (3:27). "Now to him who works, the wages are not counted as grace but as debt. But to the one who does not work but believes in the one who justifies the ungodly, his faith is accounted for righteousness…" (4:4-5).

So we have two principles or "laws" at work, which in Galatians 4 Paul actually calls "two covenants": a covenant of law, which promises blessing upon perfect obedience and curses for any transgression, and a covenant of promise, which promises blessing as a gift resulting from the personal performance of another. Since the fall, all biblical covenants serve God's redemptive purposes in Christ, who is not only prefigured but is actually embraced by our Old Testament fathers and mothers. For this reason we are wise to follow the language of the Westminster Confession: "This covenant [of grace] was differently administered in the time of the law and in the time of the gospel," as shadows give way to the reality. There have never been two plans of salvation or two peoples of God, but only one covenant of grace "under various dispensations." However, in its old covenant administration, an additional covenant was added: namely, a national covenant establishing a temporal theocracy, with Moses as the mediator, and law as its basis. The Sinai covenant is in service to the covenant of grace, establishing a divine regime for prefiguring Christ. Yet it is not itself an everlasting promise depending on Christ's sole mediation; nor does it include a remnant of all the nations, but is exclusive of Israel. The stipulations and sanctions of this covenant as spelled out, for example, in Leviticus 26 and Deuteronomy 28 (see also Joshua 24) are exactly as the Confession describes the covenant of works, "wherein life" — in this case, "long life in the land," not everlasting blessedness — "was promised to Adam" — in this case, to Israel — "upon condition of perfect and personal obedience."

Moses himself was justified by grace alone through faith in Christ alone, but the formula coined by E. P. Sanders for "covenantal nomism" is appropriate for the theocracy: "get in by grace, stay in by obedience." After the fall, God's blessings can only be a gracious gift. Delivered from Egyptian slavery by Yahweh, the "mixed multitude" that God led through the Red Sea and the desert could in no way merit the gift of Canaan (Deut. 9:5-6). However, the covenant code in Deuteronomy makes it perfectly clear that the terms for remaining God's holy nation, and avoiding eviction, were conditioned on the nation's performance of the law's stipulations.

As Jewish scholars like Jon Levinson have pointed out, the Sinai covenant and the history that emerges from it echo explicitly the imagery of a new creation, with Canaan as a new trial, and Israel as a new Adam. The temple imagery itself is replete with references to Eden, with the priests representing the people as "a royal priesthood, a holy nation, a people for God's own possession." The warning of exile, too, completes the circuit of the Adamic trial. "But like Adam they transgressed the covenant; there they dealt faithlessly with me" (Hos. 6:7). The tragedy is that Israel, like the nations, is "in Adam," yet this is also the opportunity for God to reveal his powerful salvation to the whole world: Jew and Gentile alike. Interestingly, Levenson contrasts the Sinai traditions with the Zion traditions (Abrahamic-Davidic-New Covenants) in terms that are remarkably close to Paul's contrast in Galatians 4 (as well as Hebrews 12). The former covenant is somewhat shaky, dependent as it is on human faithfulness, and it is temporal — pertaining to a piece of real estate; the latter is "above," its blessings beyond the reach of Israel's attainment, a sheer promise that in spite of disobedience God will act in saving mercy.

Covenant theology can either contribute to the confusion that Paul recognized in Galatia or alleviate it, depending on the specific kind of covenant theology being articulated. Even non-Reformed biblical scholars specializing in the treaty-covenants of the Ancient Near East emphasize the difference in form and content between law-covenants and promise-covenants in the biblical text. Indeed, Pope Benedict XVI makes the same observation, drawing on this research. So it is ironic when some recent Reformed theologians reduce these different arrangements to a single type of covenant — in essence, confusing law and gospel (whether by assimilating the former to the latter or vice versa).

In an effort to offer a biblical-theological definition, we have to go back behind Paul's famous allegory of the two mothers and try to discern the Old Testament background. While there are certainly more than two explicit covenants in scripture, they can all be grouped around two *kinds* of arrangements: conditional covenants that impose obligations and unconditional covenants that announce a divine promise. In Galatians 3, Paul labored the point that the Sinai covenant could not annul the Abrahamic promise. He treats the former as an intermezzo or parenthesis in redemptive history. The new covenant is not an extension of the Sinai covenant, but the realization of the Abrahamic covenant which the Mosaic economy foreshadowed but could never bring about.

When the prophets bring Yahweh's lawsuit, the threats are based on the covenant of law (Sinai), but beyond the exile there is the promise of a new creation, an inheritance by grace alone in the Messiah, that will include the whole earth and a remnant from all the nations. These evangelical promises look back to the Abrahamic covenant and forward to the new. None of these everlasting blessings is premised on the people's renewal of the Sinai covenant, but on Zion descending from heaven. Their performance condemns them to exile, but God's performance in the last days will bring a salvation far greater in depth and scope than the nation had experienced in its most joyful days. While Israel swore, "All this we will do," at Mount Sinai, Yahweh promises that *he* will swear a "new covenant." It is "*not like* the covenant" at Sinai (Jer 31:31-32, emphasis added). It will be God's unilateral gift of a new heart that loves his law, based on his saving presence in mercy. "'…they shall all know me, from the least of them to the greatest,' declares the LORD. 'For I will forgive their iniquity, and I will remember their sin no more'" (v 34). This covenant, God adds, is as inviolable and unbreakable as the laws of nature (vv 35-36).

Paul is therefore not introducing any new scheme that was not already present in the form and content of these treaties themselves, referred to in the prophets, executed in the ministry of John the Baptist and consummately in our Lord's ministry. It is not those who are "of the law" who are heirs, but the children of promise who are Abraham's offspring. Executing the covenant curses on the nation and its leadership, even on the temple itself, Jesus assumes the role not only of prophet but of true Israel, temple, high priest, and king upon his arrival on the temple mount to accomplish everything and claim his victory.

So Paul is treading familiar territory when he too distinguishes sharply between two types of covenants — even calling them "two covenants." Furthermore, he correlates these two covenants with "law" and "promise" as their respective basis. The further contrast Paul draws in Galatians 4 drives the point home: Sarah the free woman vs. Hagar the slave; the Jerusalem that is above vs. the Jerusalem that is below; Sinai vs. Zion. A similar contrast, especially to the last, is found in Hebrews 12:22-24.

This distinction between two types of covenants — law and promise (or gospel) — is not an imposition of systematic categories, but arises from the text itself. Rather, it is the rejection of any such distinction that seems more evidently driven by *a priori* considerations. Given the enormous consensus of non-Reformed biblical scholars, it seems hardly an opportune moment for Reformed theologians to discard the two-covenant scheme that is intrinsic to its system of doctrine.

Reformed Interpretation of the Law-Gospel Distinction

Calvin and Melanchthon were friends and colleagues. In fact, they reached such agreement on the Supper that Melanchthon earned the label "crypto-Calvinist" from Gnesio-Lutheran critics. Calvin identified himself as a disciple of Luther. It has been said many times before, but bears repeating: first, that Calvin cannot be easily distilled by searching the index of the *Institutes*. As he himself pointed out, he leaves extended exegetical arguments to his commentaries. Second, Calvin was not the only shaper of the Reformed tradition. Nevertheless, his significance is obvious enough, especially to the extent that his "paradigm" is contrasted with that of Luther and Lutheranism.

The Genevan reformer followed Thomas Aquinas in distinguishing among the civil, ceremonial, and moral aspects of the law. Through Moses God gave the law to Israel, "not to be proclaimed among all nations and to be in force everywhere." Since "the law of God which we call the moral law is nothing else than a testimony of natural law…," the common laws of nations should be ruled by equity (justice tempered by love). "Hence, this equity alone must be the goal and rule and limit of all laws, …howsoever they may differ from the Jewish law, or among themselves."

Calvin nowhere picks a fight with Luther over the law-gospel distinction. Rather, he aims his sharpest rebukes toward Roman Catholic confusion of law and gospel in relation to justification and Anabaptist tendencies to separate the Old and New Testaments. On one hand, especially in their polemics against including children of believers in baptism, Calvin held that Anabaptists disparaged the Old Testament, as if our forebears in the faith did not share with us in the same covenant of grace. Here Calvin, like Bullinger and others, stressed the unity of the covenant across both Testaments — as the Westminster Confession does above (VII.6). On the other hand, at least radical Anabaptists "deny that a commonwealth is duly framed which neglects the political system of Moses, and is ruled by the common laws of nations. Let other men consider how perilous and seditious this notion is; it will be enough for me to have proved it false and foolish." When interpreting Calvin and other Reformed writers (as well as our confessions), it is important always to bear in mind which audience is in view when continuity (one covenant of grace) or discontinuity (different administrations) is being stressed.

But did Calvin embrace Luther's law-gospel distinction, or did he affirm a more "covenantal" approach that harmonized them in terms of promise and fulfillment? Not even in this case did Calvin set out to create a new theory. However, at this point he followed Luther's critical departure from medieval interpretation. In fact, Luther's departure was in large measure a rediscovery of Augustine's, *The Spirit and the Letter*. For Aquinas, the gospel (synonymous with the New Testament) is "the new law," superior to the old law because it brings the realities to which the typological shadows merely pointed and also because it is more gracious.

Like Luther, Calvin challenged the identification of the good news as "a new law" and Christ as a new Moses. However, by distinguishing more carefully than Luther that this opposition is not between Moses and Christ *per se* or the Old and New Testaments, Calvin made room for affirming both the continuity of law and gospel (in terms of Old and New Testaments) and opposition (in terms of justification).

For the most part, Luther focused on the antithesis in doctrinal terms, as roughly equivalent to justification by works and justification through faith alone. Distinguishing law and gospel, he argued, was the chief burden of a theologian and pastors as well as the most difficult thing to do in actual practice. The law commands and threatens punishment without mercy; the gospel gives and freely absolves sinners through faith alone. The law, whether adumbrated in the Old or the New Testament, comes to kill the sinner, not to heal and reform. *Legis semper accusat*: "The law always accuses," Luther insisted. Sometimes it seems that the law and the gospel float above the actual history of redemption, as abstract principles, rather than being grounded in specific covenants. "Law" functions differently in a covenant of works ("Do this and you shall live!") than it does in a covenant of grace ("This is how the justified must live!").

Like Melanchthon, Calvin continued to speak of law and gospel in two senses: (1) as referring to the Old Testament and New Testament and (2) as referring to condemnation and justification. This important nuance is found explicitly even in Paul, where he refers to "law" in both of these senses even in the same sentence: "But now the righteousness of God has been manifested *apart from the law*, although *the Law and the Prophets* bear witness to it… (Rom. 3:21, emphasis added). Calvin himself acknowledges these two senses: "Paul harmonizes law and faith, and yet sets the righteousness of one in opposition to that of the other." Why? "The law has a twofold meaning; it sometimes includes the whole of what has been taught by Moses, and sometimes that part only which was peculiar to his ministration, which consisted of precepts, rewards, and punishments." The goal of his ministry was to lead the people of God "to despair as to their own righteousness, that they might flee to the haven of divine goodness, and so to Christ himself. This was the end or design of the Mosaic dispensation.... And whenever the word law is thus strictly taken, Moses is by implication opposed to Christ: and then we must consider what the law contains, as separate from the gospel."

This nuance is crucial for understanding the different references to law and gospel not only in Calvin but in Scripture itself. So when we dip into the *Institutes* for quotes, we should be cautioned that Calvin (again, like Luther and Melanchthon) uses "law" and "gospel" differently — and without notice, depending on the context and the point he is making.

Calvin speaks exactly like Luther when engaging Rome: law and gospel are entirely opposed. In this sense, law and gospel refer to different principles of obtaining salvation (correlative later to "covenant of works" and "covenant of grace."). Here, there is no law in the gospel and no gospel in the law. When his sights are aimed at the Anabaptists, he stresses the continuity of the law and the gospel as Old and New Testaments in one covenant of grace. Here, of course, there is gospel in the Law and the Prophets and law in the New Testament.

When it comes to the basis of salvation, Calvin is a "Lutheran." Here are some examples: In Romans 10:8, Paul's object is once again "to show how great is the difference between the righteousness of the law and that of the gospel." He adds,

> Sufficient then for pacifying minds, and for rendering certain our salvation, is the word of the gospel; in which we are not commanded to earn righteousness by works, but to embrace it, when offered gratuitously, by faith. The 'word of faith' is to be taken for the word of promise, that is, for the gospel itself, because it bears relation to faith. The contrast by which the difference between the law and the gospel appears, is indeed to be understood: and from this distinction we learn that as the law demands works, so the gospel requires nothing else, but that men bring faith to receive the grace of God. "The contrast

between Law and Gospel is to be understood, and from this distinction we deduce that, just as the Law demands work, the Gospel requires only that men should bring faith in order to receive the grace of God.

The law is a mirror, to show us our sin and send us to Christ: "This was the purpose of the ministry of Moses." The law tells us simply "what we owe" God, "according us no hope of life unless we fulfill every part of it, and, on the contrary, annexing a curse if we are guilty of the smallest transgression." "The life of the Law is man's death."

For one thing, he declares in his commentary on John, "The peculiar office of the Law [is] to summon consciences to the judgment-seat of God." The law's purpose is not to incline our hearts to godliness, but to reveal our misery so that we would flee to Christ. "Moses had no other intention than to invite all men to go straight to Christ." In his preface to the commentary on the Pentateuch he says that the whole purpose of the old covenant law is "to shut us up deprived of all confidence in our own righteousness, so that we may learn to embrace his Covenant of Grace, and flee to Christ, who is the end of the law."

In Galatians 4:24, Calvin writes, "Paul compares the two *diathekai* to two mothers.... As in the house of Abraham there were two mothers, so are there also in the Church of God. Doctrine is the mother of whom we are born, and is twofold, Legal and Evangelical," the one leading to bondage and the other to freedom. "The two covenants, then, are the mothers, of whom children unlike one another are born; for the legal covenant makes slaves, and the evangelical covenant makes freemen." In this explicit distinction between legal covenant and evangelical covenant we discern the embryonic features of the law-gospel distinction worked out in two distinct types of covenants (works and grace).

Calvin even echoes Luther's famous maxim, "The law always accuses" — for example, in a sermon on Isaiah 53:11:

> The Law only begets death; it increases our condemnation and inflames the wrath of God.... The Law of God

speaks, but it does not reform our hearts. God may show us: 'This is what I demand of you,' but if all our desires, our dispositions and thoughts are contrary to what he commands, not only are we condemned, but, as I have said, the Law makes us more culpable before God.... For in the Gospel God does not say, 'You must do this or that,' but 'believe that my only Son is your Redeemer; embrace his death and passion as the remedy for your ills; plunge yourself beneath his blood and it will be your cleansing.

Otto Weber notes the inheritance from Augustine at this point, especially his *De Spiritu et litera*: "As the Reformers saw it, Paul was really understood here...[as] the distinction between law and Gospel, between the letter and the spirit, was brought to full theological validity."

Calvin presupposes this distinction when he follows the apostles (e.g., Rom. 1:16; 10:17; 1 Pet. 1:23-25) in attributing the new birth to the preaching of the gospel. Indeed, Calvin says, "Faith is not produced by every part of the Word of God, for the warnings, admonitions and threatened judgments will not instill the confidence and peace requisite for true faith." As I. John Hesselink summarizes, "The evangelical, not the legal, character of Calvin's concept of God is what stands in the foreground." Arguing along similar lines, B. B. Warfield went so far as to suggest that Luther and Lutheranism give more place to fear in piety than we find in Calvin.

When discussing the "fatherly indulgence of God," Calvin explains Paul's reference to "the spirit of bondage" versus "the spirit of adoption," in Romans 8:15:

One he calls the spirit of bondage, which we are able to derive from the Law; and the other, the spirit of adoption, which proceeds from the Gospel. The first, he states, was formerly given to produce fear; the other is given now to afford assurance. The certainty of our salvation, which he wishes to confirm, appears, as we see, with greater clarity from such a comparison of opposites... From the adverb again we learn that Paul is here comparing the Law with the Gospel. This is the inestimable benefit which the Son of God has brought us by his advent, that we should no longer be bound by the servile condition of the Law... Although the covenant of grace is contained in the Law [now referring to it as Old Testament], yet Paul removes it from there, for in opposing the Gospel to the Law [in the theological sense] he regards only what was peculiar to the Law itself, viz. command and prohibition, and the restraining of transgressors by the threat of death. He assigns to the Law its own quality, by which it differs from the Gospel.

Therefore, there is no graciousness in the Law, as considered in itself (i.e., as a theological-hermeneutical category), but there is graciousness in the Old Testament, as the covenant of grace is promulgated in both Testaments under distinct administrations.

A distinction is made between the *totus lex* and the *nuda lex*, the former referring to the entire Old Testament, while the latter refers to the Law as a category of command without promise. But Calvin is not finished with this point:

Finally, the Law, considered in itself, can do nothing but bind those who are subject to its wretched bondage by the horror of death as well, for it promises no blessing except on condition, and pronounces death on all transgressors. As, therefore, under the Law there was the spirit of bondage, which oppressed the conscience with fear, so under the Gospel there is the spirit of adoption, which gladdens our souls with the testimony of our salvation. Note that Paul connects fear with bondage, since the Law can do nothing but harass and torment our souls with wretched discontent as long as it exercises its dominion. There is, therefore, no other remedy for pacifying our souls than when God forgives us our sins, and deals kindly with us as a father with his children.

Commenting on Galatians 3, the reformer adds,

It is an argument from *contradictions*, for the same fountain cannot yield both hot and cold. The Law holds all men under its curse. From the Law, therefore, it is useless to seek a blessing. He calls them of the works of the law who put their trust for salvation in those works. Such modes of expression must always be interpreted by the state of the question. Now we know that the controversy here relates to the cause of righteousness.... The Law justifies him who fulfills all its commands, whereas faith justifies those who are destitute of the merit of works and rely on Christ alone. To be justified by our own merit and by the grace of another are irreconcilable; *the one is overthrown by the other* (emphasis added).

If we are asking about justification, Calvin says, we must turn our attention entirely to the gospel. "If consciences wish to attain any certainty in this matter, they ought to give no place to the law." Commenting on Romans 3:21, Calvin insists that even believers after they are justified must be vigilant in distinguishing the law and gospel; otherwise, they will, with Augustine, conclude that the righteousness that they have before God, though a gift of regenerating grace alone, is inherent in the believer. "But it is evident from the context that the apostle includes all works without exception, even those which the Lord produces in his own people."

It is not enough to attribute sanctification to grace; in this whole matter, all righteousness (produced by God or self) that is by Law is to be considered the very antithesis of the righteousness that is by faith. "In the same way, in his Epistle to the Galatians he sets the Law in opposition to faith with regard to the effect of justification, because the Law promises life to those who do what it commands (Gal.2:16), and requires not only outward performance of works, but also a sincere love of God." Believer no less than the unbeliever must have the Gospel "daily repeated in the Church." "That peace of conscience, which is disturbed on the score of works, is not a one-day phenomenon, but ought to continue through our whole life." Since we are ever-assaulted by the fear inculcated by the law, we must be ever-assured of the promises of the Gospel. Whenever the believer seeks assurance or favor with God, the Law is never a comfort, but when he is trusting in Christ's imputed righteousness, his relation to the Law changes. It no longer represents God as Judge, but God as Father. Not even the justified and renewed believer can appeal to the law for assurance of God's favor.

Therefore this thing alone remains: that from the goodness of the promises he should the better judge his own misery, while with the hope of salvation cut off he thinks himself threatened with certain death. On the other hand, horrible threats hang over us, constraining and entangling not a few of us only, but all of us to a man. They hang over us, I say, and pursue us with inexorable harshness, so that we discern in the Law only the most immediate death.

The law covenants conditionally, while the Gospel covenants on the basis of Christ's fulfillment of all conditions in the believer's stead. "The promises of the Law depend on the conditions of works while the Gospel promises are free and dependent solely on God's mercy." In short, the gospel is "the instrument of regeneration and offers to us a free reconciliation with God."

The law, on the other hand, as it simply prescribes the rule of a good life, does not renew men's hearts to the obedience of righteousness, and denounces everlasting death upon transgressors, can do nothing but condemn. Or, if you prefer it another way, the office of the law is to show us the disease, in such a way as to show us, at the same time, no hope of cure: the office of the gospel is to bring a remedy to those who were past hope.

Yet this is precisely why the third use is "the principal use": since we are no longer "under the law" in the judicial sense (i.e., a covenant of law). The law can no more justify than can it sanctify. However, whereas for Luther the emphasis falls almost exclusively on the negative (condemning) function, for Calvin there is a greater sensitivity to the new relation of the believer to God and his law. Immediately after warning against giving any place to the law in assuring the conscience, Calvin adds, "Nor can any man rightly infer from this that the law is superfluous for believers, since it does not stop teaching and exhorting and urging them to do good, even though before God's judgment seat it has not place in their conscience." It is possible to delight in the law precisely because it cannot terrify the conscience of those in Christ and because through this union they are not only justified but renewed by the gospel. "For the law is not now acting toward us as a rigorous enforcement officer who is not satisfied unless the requirements are met," but is pointing out "the goal toward which throughout life we are to strive."

In short, while Calvin does indeed allow more of a "covenantal" space for the redemptive-historical transition from law (promise) to gospel (fulfillment), as Lillback and Garcia suggest, it does not keep him from making the most "Lutheran" statements about the law-gospel antithesis on the point of justification with repeated emphasis. He is not self-contradictory on the point unless we fail to follow his own rule of distinguishing between law-gospel continuity in relation to Old and New Testaments and law-gospel contrast in relation to Christ with his benefits.

In my view, Calvin (among others) improved on Luther's principle. In addition to widening the scope to accommodate greater nuance demanded by actual passages, Calvin's subtle but important differences from Lutheran treatments bear a richer redemptive-historical and eschatological flavor. In fact, where divergences appear even implicitly, they are due more to this than to any formal difference over the distinction itself. I do not have space to pursue the point adequately, but perhaps I may be allowed to summarize briefly.

Luther seems more dialectical in his thinking (e.g., old man wholly condemned and sinful; new man wholly justified and renewed), often leading to a somewhat abstract opposition to law and gospel in principle. So in this dialectical view, it is easy to exaggerate in both extremes. On one hand, there is a somewhat over-realized eschatology:

> Oh, it is a living, busy, active, mighty thing, this faith. And so it is impossible for it not to do good works incessantly. It does not ask whether there are good works to

do, but before the question rises, it has already done them, and is always at the doing of them.... Hence a man is ready and glad, without compulsion, to do good to everyone, to serve everyone, to suffer everything, in love and praise to God, who has shown him this grace. And thus it is impossible to separate works from faith, quite as impossible as to separate burning and shining from fire.

On the other hand, Luther can say, "I have heard of it but as yet have seen nothing of it. Not in essence, but by promise, I have eternal life. I have it in obscurity, I do not see it, but I believe it and will hereafter surely feel it."

Calvin thinks more redemptive-historically and eschatologically. In Reformed theology, the believer is not *in any sense* the "old man" who is "under the law" as a covenant, but has passed from condemnation to justification, from death to life. There is a definitive transition here; the new creation has dawned. Believers are not only forgiven and justified, but definitively transformed.

Thus, their relation to the law has changed forever and they do experience this reality. At the same time, they do not simply do good works spontaneously with uninterrupted zeal. Although the believer is definitively baptized into the new creation (Rom 6), he or she at the same time struggles with doubt and indwelling sin (Rom 7), confident that the one in whom we are justified and renewed will also glorify us in the future as part of a restored creation (Rom 8). Thus, the subject of this paradox is not divided between two existing personas, but the Pauline formula of the "old/new self" is a way of referring to the eschatological tension between the still fallen character of our existence in this age and the new creation into which the Spirit has inserted us, with all of the penetrating powers of the age to come breaking in upon the justified sinner. From this perspective, an *already-not yet* tension seems sometimes threatened in Lutheran theology by a *both-and* dialectic.

This new relation of the believer to the law is why the "third use" is the "principal use" for Calvin: precisely because the law cannot condemn those who cling to Christ alone in faith. The same is true of the tradition generally. The law still shows us what our sins deserve so that we will desert lingering confidence in our own "righteousness" and flee to Christ (WCF XIX.6). Yet because of this definitive transition in history between old and new creation with Christ's resurrection from the dead, the law can only show us what God requires and forbids, "although not as due to them by the law as a covenant of works" (*ibid.*).

However, even in suggesting such differences, I am reminded of many statements in Luther where law and gospel are treated with nuance (refusing, for example, to identify them with Old and New Testaments, respectively); the definitive breach with sin's power as well as its guilt is maintained vigorously. Calvin agrees with Luther not only that the law cannot justify but that only the Gospel promises can move us to grateful obedience: "He lays hold not only of the precepts," says Calvin, "but the accompanying promise of grace, which alone sweetens what is bitter. For what would be less lovable than the Law if, with importuning and threatening alone, it troubles souls through fear, and distressed them through fright? David especially shows that in the Law he apprehended the Mediator, without whom there is no delight or sweetness."

Furthermore, not only is the "third use" of the law (obliging believers to walk in holiness) affirmed extensively and vigorously in the Book of Concord; Luther's treatise *Against the Antinomians* argued that this heresy was as dangerous in separating sanctification from justification — as if to tear Christ into pieces — as Rome's assimilation of the latter to the former. It was Melanchthon who first introduced the "three uses of the law." Hesselink's conclusion suffices: "Here Calvin does not differ significantly from Luther, except in emphasis and discretion."

Does the Reformed Tradition Develop Calvin's Law-Gospel Hermeneutic?

While it is anachronistic to read later refinements into Calvin, it is clear enough that he not only held to a distinction between law and gospel, but that he characterized them (with Paul) as two distinct covenants: legal and evangelical. In fact, the way of works is "a covenant of law." Furthermore, he held to what would be identified as "the active obedience" of Christ. "A man who was free, by constituting himself a surety, redeems a slave: by putting on himself the chains, he takes them off from the other. So Christ chose to become liable to keep the law, that exemption from it might be obtained for us..." — exemption, that is, from its threat, but not from its moral authority.

The influences of Luther and Melanchthon on Reformed leaders were hardly limited to Calvin. Melanchthon's *Loci communes* was influential in Bullinger's renunciation of his decision to join the Carthusians and become a "Martinist" (follower of Luther), and Calvin translated the *Loci* into French. Ursinus studied under Melanchthon at Wittenberg before he adopted the Reformed confession. In spite of the Eucharistic controversy, where differences were clearly debated, the law-gospel distinction was never among the disputed points. It appears in Bullinger's *Second Helvetic Confession*. Wilhelm Niesel observes, "Reformed theology recognises the contrast between Law and Gospel, in a way similar to Lutheranism. We read in the Second Helvetic Confession: 'The Gospel is indeed opposed to the Law. For the Law works wrath and pronounces a curse, whereas the Gospel preaches grace and blessing.'" As Otto Weber points out, in Heidelberg, Herborn, Marburg and Bremen, all places where the Reformed movement was strongly influenced by Melanchthon, the concept of the covenant came to dominate dogmatics, even subordinating predestination to it. If some today are wary of "Lutheranizing" influences, the whole tradition seems rather compromised in that regard.

While some have sought to separate Calvin from Luther, some of their professed heirs have sought to separate both from Calvinism and Lutheranism. In recent Reformed developments, no figure is more the target of such caricatures than Theodore Beza, Calvin's close associate and hand-picked successor. Furthermore, Beza explicitly carried on Calvin's work and no better can this consistency be observed than in Beza's *Confessio*, published in Geneva in 1558.

In that summary of the faith, Beza addresses "The means which the Holy Spirit uses to create faith in the heart of the elect." His answer, of course, is the Word and the sacraments, and these discussions therefore follow. But the discussion of "The Word" itself is divided into two parts: "The Law" and "The Gospel."

> We divide this Word into two principal parts or kinds: the one is called the 'Law,' the other the 'Gospel.' For, all the rest can be gathered under one or the other of these two headings. What we call Law (when it is distinguished from Gospel and is taken for one of the two parts of the Word) is a doctrine whose seed is written by nature in our hearts... What we call the Gospel ('Good News') is a doctrine which is not at all in us by nature, but which is revealed from Heaven (Mt.16:17; Jn.1:13), and totally surpasses natural knowledge. By it God testifies to us that it is his purpose to save us freely by his only Son (Rom.3:20-22), provided that, by faith, we embrace him as our only wisdom, righteousness, sanctification and redemption (1Cor.1:30).

Beza warns, "We must pay great attention to these things. For, with good reason, we can say that ignorance of this distinction between Law and Gospel is one of the principal sources of the abuses which corrupted and still corrupt Christianity." Why is this? People always turn the Law into something easy and the Gospel into something difficult, as if the Gospel were "nothing other than a second Law, more perfect than the first." Beza then devotes a great deal of space to distinguishing the Law from the Gospel. We know the law by nature, inwardly, while the Gospel is "from above." "Having carefully understood this distinction of the two parts of the Word of God, the Law and the Gospel, it is easy to understand how and to what end the Holy Spirit uses the preaching of the one and the other in the Church." We do not know our sinfulness. "This is why God begins with the preaching of the Law," and after discussing this point more fully, he concludes, "There then is the first use of the preaching of the Law." But "after the Law comes the Gospel" in preaching. The "third use" Beza discusses under the heading, "The other fruit of the preaching of the Law, once the preaching of the Gospel has effectually done its work," and here he argues that because the believer's relation to the Law has changed, it simply directs instead of inspiring fear and doubt.

This distinction between law and gospel is just as prominent in the writings of Reformed theologians as diverse as Zacharius Ursinus, William Perkins, and John Owen. In fact, as I have argued elsewhere, it is the substratum on which the federal system of the covenant of works and the covenant of grace is overlaid.

Continental Development

As early as the first page of his *Commentary on the Heidelberg Catechism*, Ursinus (primary author of the *Heidelberg Catechism*) states, "The doctrine of the church is the entire and uncorrupted doctrine of the law and gospel concerning the true God, together with his will, works, and worship." He then elucidates what was to be a typical Reformed statement of the distinction that was held in common with the Lutheran confession:

> The doctrine of the church consists of two parts: the Law, and the Gospel; in which we have comprehended the sum and substance of the sacred Scriptures.... Therefore, the law and gospel are the chief and general divisions of holy scriptures, and comprise the entire doctrine comprehended therein ... for the law is our schoolmaster, to bring us to Christ, constraining us to fly to him, and showing us what that righteousness is, which he has wrought out, and now offers unto us. But the gospel, professedly, treats of the person, office, and benefits of Christ. Therefore we have, in the law and gospel, the whole of the Scriptures comprehending the doctrine revealed from heaven for our salvation.... The law prescribes and enjoins what is to be done, and forbids what ought to be avoided: whilst the gospel announces the free remission of sin, through and for the sake of Christ.... The law is known from nature; the gospel is divinely revealed.

Ursinus was hardly a crypto-Lutheran, having converted to the Reformed confession, and his view had already been amplified by Bullinger and Calvin, two figures in the tradition who were widely known to disagree from time to time — especially over the latter's perceived Lutheran sympathies.

A trail of the formative Reformed theologians not only invoked the distinction, but made it integral to their covenant theology. They warn repeatedly of turning the gospel into a new law, of confusing law and gospel, and especially of denying the covenant of works as the counterpart to the covenant of grace. Peter van Mastricht cautioned that such confusion would undermine the active obedience of Christ and therefore imputed justification. In fact, he adds that in Hebrews 2:14-15 "the Apostle is speaking of the covenant in Paradise so far as it is re-enacted and renewed with Israel at Sinai in the Decalogue, which contained the proof of the covenant of works. In the words of the Formula Consensus Helvetica, "the promise annexed to the covenant of works was not just the continuation of earthly life and felicity," but of a confirmation in righteousness and everlasting heavenly joy.

Herman Witsius's widely influential *Economy of the Covenants* (1677) reflects the consensus in organizing Scripture according to its own internal distinction between law and gospel, a covenant of works and a covenant of grace. Even those who found themselves on opposite sides in many debates, like Cocceius and Voetius, jointly emphasized the absolute and unconditional foundation of the covenant and saw the law-gospel distinction as integral for its preservation. "Ypeij and Dermout point out that in those days a denial of the covenant of works was regarded as a heresy," Berkhof observes. A confusion at this point would mean a confusion of law and gospel — the very confusion that Paul lamented in Romans 10 concerning his fellow-Jews and criticized with such vehemence in his letter to the Galatians.

The continental Reformed theologians during and immediately following the Reformation period were unanimous in this respect and the significant structural place that they give to "Law and Gospel" in their systems is evident even as recently as Louis

Berkhof's opening to his section "The Word of God as a Means of Grace." J. Van Bruggen adds more recently,

> The [*Heidelberg*] *Catechism*, thus, mentions the gospel and deliberately does not speak of 'the Word of God,' because the Law does not work faith. The Law (Law and gospel are the two parts of the Word which may be distinguished) judges; it does not call a person to God and does not work trust in him. The gospel does that.

Puritan Development

We cannot even find a basis for separating the Puritans from their Continental counterparts, especially since the Westminster Confession was the culmination of these British labors. The divines appealed liberally to Robert Rollock, a pioneer of federal theology, who explicitly develops the two-covenant scheme out of the law-gospel distinction. William Perkins, father of Elizabethan Puritanism, taught practical theology to generations of students through his *Art of Prophesying* (1592, 1606). In that work he asserts, "The basic principle in application is to know whether the passage is a statement of the law or of the gospel. For when the Word is preached, the law and the gospel operate differently. The law exposes the disease of sin, and as a side-effect stimulates and stirs it up. But it provides no remedy for it.... The law is, therefore, first in the order of teaching; then comes the gospel." We must be attentive, he says, to the ways in which even inspired Old Testament expressions of law are made in the New Testament inspired expressions of gospel. He cites Deuteronomy 20:11, 14: "For this commandment which I command you today is not too mysterious for you, nor is it far off.... But the word is very near you, in your mouth and in your heart, that you may do it." "This same sentence which is legal in character in Moses," Perkins points out, "is evangelical in character in Paul (Rom. 10:8)." Even believers need to hear the Bible preached and applied with a clear view of this distinction. "Our sanctification is partial as yet. In order that the remnants of sin may be destroyed we must always begin with meditation on the law, and with a sense of our sin, in order to be brought to rest in the gospel."

Though Reformed divines were convinced that the covenant of grace is unconditionally gracious in its basis, they acknowledged that it also included conditions. These were not conditions in the strict sense (as in a covenant of works), since even repentance and faith were gracious gifts. Every covenant involves two parties. Apart from faith, there is no justification, and apart from works, there is no faith. Union with Christ brings justification and sanctification through the same act of faith. Again, all of this can be found in Luther and his heirs as well. However, just as Lutheran pietism emphasized the subjective and conditional character of this union, Puritanism developed some of its own antinomian-neonomian debates.

Concerned about a growing lack of assurance in the gospel among some, Petrus Dathenus, author of the Dutch Reformed liturgy adopted at the Convent of Wessels, wrote a winsome little dialogue with an English noblewoman. His *Pearl of Christian Comfort* takes as its main thesis that its interlocutor did not know how to properly distinguish law and gospel because of the moralistic preaching to which she was being exposed.

But all along, a clear trajectory emerges: those who emphasized a distinction between the covenant of works and covenant of grace (law and gospel) discerned in their fellow-churchmen who blurred that distinction nothing less than the spirit of Arminian neonomianism or Romish legalism. Exchanges became heated, for example between John Owen and Thomas Goodwin over against Richard Baxter and John Goodwin. According to the former pair, rejection of the classic formulation of covenant theology seemed to go hand-in-hand with a rejection of a purely forensic justification.

The Marrow Controversy in Scotland, in which a rediscovered theology text from 1645 by Edward Fisher that had been celebrated by its contemporaries was vilified as "antinomian" by an eighteenth-century Church of Scotland that indicted unblemished Puritan fathers such as John Preston as being antinomian for regarding salvation entirely as "a deed of gift and grant." Eventuating in the Secession of 1733, the controversy shows that the dominant sentiments in the Church of

Scotland in that period were so far removed from those of the Reformation that the standard Reformed orthodoxy enshrined in the Westminster Standards could be condemned as antinomian heresy.

This law-gospel/covenant of works-covenant of grace structure is far from idiosyncratic, but represents the organic development of Reformed, covenant theology. This pattern of rendering "law-gospel" and "covenant of works-covenant of grace" interchangeable is not a Lutheran-Calvinist hybrid imposed recently on Reformed theology. Any typical manual of confessional teaching from any writer in our tradition before World War II elucidated this scheme.

With no suspicion that it downplays the *historia salutis* in favor of the *ordo salutis*, Geerhardus Vos treats the covenant of works-grace scheme as a corollary of the law-gospel distinction. In fact, he observes that Reformed theologians "who strictly separate law and gospel and make the latter to consist wholly of promises — as a matter of fact, those theologians more than others — put emphasis on the fact that the law, as the comprehensive norm for the life of man, also determines man's relation to the gospel." It is Christ's fulfillment of the covenant of works that gives solidity to the covenant of grace. "The covenant is neither a hypothetical relationship, nor a conditional position; rather it is the fresh, living fellowship in which the power of grace is operative."

Drawing heavily on Turretin, Charles Hodge repeats the same structure. For example, in relation to promise-and-fulfillment, the old covenant belongs to the gospel (covenant of grace) by type and shadow. Yet he adds, the form and content of the national covenant sworn at Sinai by the people is "a legal covenant," with Moses as the mediator. In this respect, it is a recapitulation of the original covenant of works with Adam.

It is in fact nothing but a declaration of the eternal and immutable principles of justice. If a man rejects or neglects the gospel, these are the principles, as Paul teaches in the opening chapters of his Epistle to the Romans, according to which he will be judged. If he will not be under grace, if he will not accede to the method of salvation by grace, he is of necessity under the law.

Similarly, in his *Commentary on Second Corinthians* he observes that the Mosaic law was, first, a "reenactment of the covenant of works" and in this sense, is a ministry of condemnation and death; second, a "national covenant" based on national obedience and "in this way it was purely legal." But thirdly, it pointed Israel to Christ. It was on this point — whether the Mosaic covenant was in some sense a reenactment of the covenant of works — that our tradition has displayed, and may understandably continue to display, some variance of positions.

Challenging the Distinction

Along with the law-gospel distinction, Karl Barth rejected the idea of a covenant of law or works that could be distinguished from the one covenant of grace. In fact, the distinction between these covenants marked the first "fatal historical moment" in Reformed theology, Barth insisted. Those who suspect the classic Calvinists of setting systematic theology (*ordo salutis*) above or even against biblical theology (*historia salutis*) might also be interested in Barth's second "fateful moment" in Reformed orthodoxy: "...the introduction of an understanding of revelation as a sequence of [historical] stages." A vigorous "Calvin versus the Calvinists" school emerged in Barth's wake.

Conclusion

Like the reformers and their heirs, Thomas Boston, at the center of the Marrow controversy, warned, "In a sinking state of the church, the law and gospel are confounded, and the law jostles out the gospel, the dark shades of morality take place of gospel light; which plague is this day begun in the church, and well far advanced." It is entirely possible to avoid Arminian or Roman Catholic conclusions about justification without accepting every element of the Reformed-covenantal system. Yet at least within our tradition, challenges to that system rarely fail to lead to further distortions of the gospel; justification eventually loses its supporting beams and buttresses.

As Reformed Christians, we believe that it is the Spirit, working through his Word, who not only unites us to Christ but to the communion of saints, so that our witness participates in what Jaroslav Pelikan called "the living tradition of the dead" rather than "the dead tradition of the living." In my own experience, the deeper I go into the Reformed tradition, the more I am challenged in my parochialism and opened up to the great conversation to which the Reformed introduce me, and is still in progress. These figures introduce us not only to deeper differences but to deeper affinities of which we were not aware. Overstating similarities would be a mistake. Yet overstating differences leads inevitably not only to caricature of other traditions, but to idiosyncratic and possibly dangerous interpretations of one's own tradition that have in fact been rejected for reasons that seem to me to have been justified by recent trajectories in Reformed as well as other circles.

It seems improbable that the glad tidings of God's free justification of sinners can be recovered again more widely in our day apart from the broader and deeper distinction between law and gospel that provides its proper exegetical context.

Law and Gospel:

Separators, Confusers and Preachers

Steven D. Paulson

As he was sitting at his table for dinner, Luther was once asked about the beginning of the Reformation and he replied, "When I discovered the distinction of law and gospel, I broke through." Broke through what? The legal scheme. The law alone. So, whatever is left of Lutherans, the evangelical cause, this is it: distinguishing law and gospel. That alone is what makes a theologian.

But the distinction of law and gospel is very hard, since it goes against our desire (even our desire for the highest good). Distinguishing law and gospel kills the preacher and the hearer, and who wants to die or kill? We just cannot desire it. So the opponents of distinguishing law and gospel are many and substantial: the soul, which does not desire it, the church tradition which fears it ever since Tertullian and Marcion, and the devil, who occupies himself wholly with this one thing — to confuse law and gospel. In the face of such enemies, distinguishing law and gospel properly is a real case of David vs. Goliath. The chances do not look good, to speak in a fleshly way.

No sooner had law and gospel appeared than Lutherans made a mess of it. So today we should feel in good company. As Jakob Andreae said, in the fifth article of the *Formula of Concord*: "a dispute arose." Imagine that, a dispute among Lutherans! That dispute is a fault line in Lutheranism and so in the whole catholic church. The trouble resulted from the attempt to make repentance into a mere self-reference, a psychology, instead of what repentance really is — a violent, cosmic withdrawal from yourself into Christ: "The law and the prophets were until John;

since then the good news of the kingdom of God is preached, and every one enters it violently" (Luke 16:16 RSV). We want to repent ourselves before God, not to be repented violently, meaning we desire to live rather than die. Who can blame us? Even when God is doing the killing, we cannot find a way to love it. The *proper use of the law* is to put you and me to death. That truth we cannot quite stomach. The *proper use of the gospel* is to raise the dead. This also seems a little more than we wanted. How about getting just a change in life; wouldn't the Spirit consider that enough of a change?

The fault line is illustrated for us by the fight between Johann Agricola and Philip Melanchthon, who are the cause of the "dispute" referred to in the fifth article of the *Formula of Concord*. Agricola shows us the one side of the problem. The law belongs in the outside world (courthouse); only the gospel belongs in the pulpit. We call these the Separators. They preach love, not wrath. The carrot, not the stick, is the way to get people to repent, otherwise people will have a bad "self-reference" and lose motivation.

On the other side of the fault line another problem arose, if not directly with Philip Melanchthon, then some of his students like Paul Crell, who said, the "*opus proprium* of the *gospel* was to make the sin great." My goodness, what a re-writing of Paul that was; the main work of the gospel is to increase your sin! But at least they knew you had to preach both law and gospel; however, the way they did so was a problem. They knew that preaching only the law does not lead to true repentance either. If a sinner is convinced of God's anger, what does a sinner do? Deny! Hide! Even Sigmund Freud will tell you that much. But they falsely concluded that law *cooperates* with the gospel in moving a person from terror to comfort.

It took Luther slogging through the Antinomian Disputations to put his finger on the issue that troubled both the Phillipists and the antinomian Agricola. The law does not cooperate with the gospel. This was quite a discovery. Law and gospel are not a process. The law is not a first step in the same direction as the gospel. They are not two mules pulling the cart in the same direction. True, the law causes you to run from the wrath of God, but it cannot get you to run in the right direction. Luther asked, is the law necessary for justification? He responded, "No. He who is made contrite by the law is far from reaching grace; he rather goes farther away from it." Luther recognized that Peter would have ended up just like Judas if a preacher was not sent. So, the law is not a first step toward salvation. The preacher interrupts whatever path the fleeing sinner is on.

This showed Luther that the Phillipists did not separate law and gospel; they *confused* them. So here are the two sides of the fault line: Separators and Confusers. The Confusers at least kept both law and gospel in preaching — so close, and yet so far away. It is like Jesus saying to the rich man: You are close to the kingdom, but not in it. So, Melanchthon's students started a logical progression that goes like this: Law produces terror, but terror must give over to another psychological state called "comfort" that comes from the gospel's promises alone. Soon faith becomes nothing more than "assent" to God's plan of using law and gospel, to move you from terror to comfort.

Law, as Decalog or Ten Commandments, starts a process of *self-knowledge* for this way of thinking. Repentance gets turned inward. They concluded that law provides a true, self-knowledge of sins, but not sin; there had to be a further step taken. In order to get to full repentance (to examine and know my whole self as sinner), the cross of Jesus Christ had to be added to Moses' tablets. When Christ was depicted to people with his suffering and crown of thorns, their hearts will finally soften. They concluded that since the cross is gospel, then evangelical repentance (knowing yourself wholly as a sinner) is *truly and properly* from the preaching of the gospel. The main job of the gospel was to get you to repent, to terrorize you, to scare hell out of you.

But then, notice what happens when you make law and gospel into a two-step process of justification. If the law cooperates with the gospel in moving persons from terror to comfort, then the old sinner remains. The preacher can only change their psychological state, their way of knowing themselves. The law comes to be understood primarily in its psychological effect. God's wrath is understood from the experience of terror — which allowed a terrible reversal. It occurs to a sinner: "If I can get rid of my feelings of terror, I have gotten rid of the wrath of God itself!"

So in the modern world, say around the time of Descartes' inward turn, people looked around and noticed something: no one is feeling any terror anymore! Actually they never did. But, preachers started to think that preaching the law is passé; it doesn't really work. The Gospel can and must be fitted to our "new context," we say. If people felt sinful, we could forgive their sins, but they do not. So forgiveness doesn't "work" as gospel. If people felt terror, we could give them comfort by telling them that God has come to make peace; but they don't feel terror. So what are we to preach?

Preachers started looking, as psychologists do, for a disease they can possibly cure. So, Lutherans in particular looked around and saw that people feel restless, nervous; they feel anxious, lonely, disconnected, and incomplete. They are bowling alone. They feel — now we can go to the main word — like they are being judged unfairly by others and not *affirmed* in their lives. What then is the gospel supposed to do in this new context? Even the greatest of the theologians of the past generation fell for this. Paul Tillich decided that if we could, -- and why can't we? — we should replace justification as a word (which is really an old medieval, scholastic thing anyway). But since it is a biblical word, we can't throw it out on that technicality. So, instead we must adapt it with the term "acceptance": "acceptance in the sense that we are accepted by God although being unacceptable according to the criteria of the law… and that we are asked to accept this acceptance."

Here we have inherited a mess: the gospel's proper work is to make sinners self-aware! Accept themselves! Once the Rubicon is crossed like this, the next step is that a person ends by mixing love with the gospel. Yet, in doing this, one ends up preaching only the law to people — as a Confuser, even though it is laced with references to love. This kind of thing is exactly what the devil loves, since he invented the game of confusing law and gospel. The result is this current pattern for sermons:

Your problem is that you don't feel loved.

But you should know God loves you — even so much as to give his Son on the cross.

Now is the time for you to respond, since love is not only a gift, but a task, so get out in the world, do the mission of God, and love one another.

Once this happens, it will not take people long to figure out that when they really want acceptance, they don't need a preacher. They can just wake up one day and apply it to themselves like BenGay! And, lo and behold, church and preaching become extraneous to my personal well-being and freedom overnight. Not only are you preachers no longer needed, in fact, preachers get in the way of my self-affirmation. Goodbye church.

Confusion is the basic problem of law and gospel today, as the fifth article of the *Formula of Concord* put it: *confusio inter legem et evangelium*. Confusion means putting the law and gospel together as two parts that make a greater whole, which confuses love with faith just as the old scholastic use of *caritas* did. But love does not save, not even the *caritas* kind; faith alone does that. Confusion does not leave a little law and a little gospel. Everything becomes law from beginning to end, even if you call it a third use.

Confusing leaves two repeated mistakes when it comes to distinguishing law and gospel; first, to take law/gospel as one "hermeneutic," or "lens," by which you interpret Scriptures. The distinction of law and gospel is not a lens. It is as the *Formula*'s fifth article rightly put it: the "bright light" of Lutheran theology. Light is not the thing you look through to see. But law and gospel is the very external light of Christ that illuminates your eye. It was why Luther broke through. The second mistake is to take law/gospel as a certain style of preaching: making people feel bad before you make them feel good.

Instead, distinguishing law and gospel is God's double work on sinners, not a theory, not a style, not a human tool. So, instead of Separators and Confusers we want Dialecticians (real preachers). By that we mean Appliers who know God does two things: kills and makes alive (1 Sam. 2). Then when we suffer these divine works, we are not continually existing subjects looking for a psychological change. We are not merely sinners learning how to repent through inward investigation. Nor are we Christians who have no old creature hanging on our necks — as if there is no sin after baptism. Instead, we have become in baptism "two you's" with an "overlap" for the time being — *simul iustus et peccator*.

The key to stop confusing law and gospel is to learn that the law has one, and only one, ending — who is Jesus Christ, and his new kingdom. Christ is the end of the law (Romans 10:4). No one and nothing else is. We are not becoming self-aware in repentance; we are being put to death and raised up new — by the sheer application to a sinner of the office of the keys. Christ "did not come to save the righteous, but the sinners" (Matt. 9:13). The way he did it was to send a preacher to forgive.

When the law is told exactly where it does not belong in the new kingdom, then it is also becomes at the same time established — as Paul says in Romans 3. That means the law is put where in fact it does belong, in its penultimate place in this old world. There law stays behind us, eternally — in our members, hands feet and appendages in the old world, or old Adam — even when it puts us to death. But law does not belong in the new world. So, as long as we remain in this old world, we preach the law, thus making God's demands crystal clear, regardless of the fact that you will not desire or like the law because it will give you no affirmation or acceptance. So here is our Lutheran slogan that you may use freely and spread widely: The law! … until Christ!

A Catholic Theology Teacher Drawing on the Lutheran Legacy

Jared Wicks, SJ

Since the mid-1960s I have drawn on portions of Luther's theological and spiritual legacy as a resource in teaching Catholic theology. I hope that the students whom I, along with my colleagues, have been forming are better ministers of word, sacrament, and of pastoral care, by reason of elements drawn from Luther which have slipped into my instruction.

Here I will interweave personal testimony with theological reflections and clarifications, beginning with my activity as professor in Jesuit schools of theology and ministry, where I taught with others who, like myself, were formed in Jesuit or Ignatian spirituality. While this spirituality marked our theology implicitly, the teaching itself — on the human person, the word of God's revelation, interpreting Scripture, Christology — was deeply marked by the legacy of the Second Vatican Council. From these two perspectives, from the Ignatian "sub-soil" and from Vatican II, I can note aspects of the law/gospel contrast and dynamic.

Then I will move on from the corporate setting of my teaching in Jesuit schools to talk about some high points of my own itinerary of study and writing on Martin Luther, making explicit what I value highly in Luther's contributions to my own Catholic theology. Finally, I will offer my assessment of the Law/Gospel distinction, with some reasons for a Catholic reluctance to adopt this element of the Lutheran heritage.

Elements of Law and Gospel in Catholic Theological Education

I worked as a theological educator at Jesuit School of Theology in Chicago from 1967 to 1979 and after that I continued in the Theology Faculty of the Gregorian University in Rome from 1979 to 2004. In both places, we professors wanted our theological program to support our students' and graduates' personal growth as faithful, prayerful, self-sacrificing disciples of Christ the Lord. We saw them as individuals responding to Jesus Christ, who was calling them to follow him as disciples and to be sent into the church as his ministers. Here spiritual formation according to the principles of Ignatius Loyola and his *Spiritual Exercises* played a supporting role, which gave our theology a particular profile.

It is relevant to this conference's topic that the Ignatian *Exercises* have their own Law/Gospel dynamic, because they begin by having the person meditate as a sinner confronted by the destructive inroads of sin in human history and personally in himself/herself. Early in a retreat according to the *Exercises*, the "light" one asks for is a sense of "shame and confusion," because Scripture shows how sin brings lives to disaster and I know that I have deserved condemnation for my own sins.[1] One prays before Jesus Christ on his Cross, marveling that he came into the world to die for our sins — there I will reflect on myself (no. 53). The sinner extols the mercy of God for granting life and forgiveness. Then as the *Exercises* further unfold, the retreatant meditates on gospel passages, gradually focusing on his response to Jesus Christ — the Lord and Savior, incarnate, suffering, and gloriously risen — who addresses followers, who know they are forgiven sinners, but find themselves graced with Christ's personal call to dedicated and costly discipleship in service for the good of the human family.

The *Spiritual Exercises*, which underlay our teaching in Chicago and at the Gregorian, have their own law/gospel dynamic,

---

1. *The Spiritual Exercises of St. Ignatius Loyola*, trans. Louis J. Puhl (Chicago: Loyola University Press, 1951), no. 48. Because of the variety of translations now in use, I cite by the paragraph number.

in moving from sin and loss, through forgiveness, to the call to discipleship by the Lord who became incarnate, willingly gave himself in death to ransom many, and rose into the life he lives now in glory and in his body the church.

In this work of education, a ministerial dimension lurks in the theology itself, for the latter looks to form ministers, especially Catholic priests, who will give a convinced and well-focused witness to God's saving work in Christ, especially as they preach from the Catholic lectionary.

The Catholic Fundamental Theology that we taught at the Gregorian was based on the Vatican II Dogmatic Constitution on Divine Revelation (*Dei Verbum*, 1965). This shining gem among the Vatican II documents offers to future ministers of the Word a visionary framework for preaching. It gives, as I read it, the central contents that a homilist can and should, in the ministry of the Word, repeatedly tease out of the lectionary passages, especially the Gospels.

Dei Verbum is clearly relevant to today's topic. It orients the formed Catholic minister of the Word to read Scripture christocentrically, especially by its comprehensive affirmation that "the truth God has revealed about himself and about human salvation shines forth for us in Christ, who is himself at the same time the mediator and the fullness (*mediator simul et plenitudo*) of the whole of revelation" (DV 2). No. 7 adds, "In Christ Jesus the entire revelation of the most high God is summed up" (*consummatur*, "is recapitulated"). This is Vatican II's christocentrism of revelation, given in *Dei Verbum*.

But *Dei Verbum* made a significant further contribution when, in no. 4, it specified and sharpened its Christology of revelation soteriologically. For Jesus Christ, in his presence and manifestation, his words and works, his signs and miracles, and above all in his death and glorious resurrection, and finally in sending the Spirit of truth — in all this — Jesus reveals "that God is with us to free us from the darkness of sin and death and to raise us to eternal life." Revelation's content is centrally *evangelium*, for Jesus Christ is present to the human family as Immanuel, as

God with us to deliver and to save. We hoped that our Gregorian graduates would have and work from this "visionary framework" when they preach and otherwise interpret the Gospels — finding in the different Gospel passages the gospel as a message of liberation from sin and death.

In these initial testimonies, I have indicated how elements of the Law/Gospel duality are present in the program of Catholic theological formation in which I have been active. But the concentrated dynamic of conversion that Law/Gospel gives to Lutherans — that you will not find. The specific Lutheran dynamic of Law/Gospel — as the basic movement of conversion — is not explicitly adopted by Catholics. I will return to this later.

Luther as a Resource in the Itinerary of One Catholic Theologian's Work

Let me begin this section with some personal history, into which I will weave insights into Luther. In 1967 I completed my dissertation on Luther's early works down to the indulgence controversy. I did this in the Catholic Theology Faculty of the University of Münster, under the guidance of Erwin Iserloh, while I also had helpful contacts with professors and students of the parallel Evangelical Faculty of the University. The dissertation became a book in 1968, which celebrates Luther on life-long penance (Thesis 1 on indulgences), noting however with emphasis the role in penance of God's "healing grace" (*gratia sanans*) — for which everyone must yearn, long, and beg each day.[2]

In the 1970s, I presented Luther at some length in the French *Dictionnaire de Spiritualité*, after which I reworked the *Dictionnaire* text for the 1983 centenary year in the book *Luther and His Spiritual Legacy*.[3]

---

2. J. Wicks, *Man Yearning for Grace. Luther's Early Spiritual Teaching* (Washington, DC, and Cleveland: Corpus Books, 1968), now out of print after the demise of Corpus Books. But it also came out under the aegis of the *Institut für europäische Geschichte*, Mainz, published in 1969 by Franz Steiner Verlag of Wiesbaden.

3. Published in Wilmington, Delaware, by Michael Glazer, Inc., a publisher now incorporated into Liturgical Press, Collegeville, Minnesota, which however has not reprinted my book.

I moved to the Gregorian in Rome in 1979, and there some of my work on Luther was welcomed for publication in our theological quarterly *Gregorianum*. A 1984 article was my *retractatio* of a critical point in my dissertation, concerning the *pro me* which I had seen as a ruinous introversion in Luther's 1518 conception of faith.[4] By 1984, I was convinced that the key notion was *fides sacramenti* — faith in the sacramental word, out of which the *pro me* emerges smoothly.[5] In 1989, *Gregorianum* brought out another article, "Living and Praying as *simul iustus et peccator*," which claimed that Catholics could very well set aside their reservations on the *simul*, for instance, the misgivings over it from the Catholic side that were inserted into the 1983 USA dialogue document, *Justification by Faith*.

All my early work on Luther — the Münster dissertation, my Dictionnaire entry, articles on *fides sacramenti* and on living as *simul iustus et peccator* — came together in the concluding chapter of *Luther and His Spiritual Legacy*, where I present "Luther's Mature Spiritual Teaching" in thirty-two pages, filled with Luther citations, including passages from his commentary on Psalm 51 on the law's inculcation of such an awareness of sin that leaves no help but that of Jesus Christ.[6] I love that chapter and still recommend it to Catholic students and seminarians, so they may come to know Luther as a comprehensive and genial teacher of Christian believing and living, especially with the *simul iustus et peccator*, which

---

4. The correction came in "*Fides sacramenti – fides specialis*: Luther's Development in 1518," *Gregorianum* 65 (1984), 481–518. Formation in the *Spiritual Exercises* should have alerted me to tread softly about the *pro me* in faith, since when Master Ignatius leads one in meditating on our Lord's nativity, a consideration is that they went to Bethlehem "so that our Lord might be born in extreme poverty, and that after many labors, after hunger, thirst, heat, and cold, after insults and outrages, he might die on the cross, and all this for me. Then I will reflect and draw some spiritual fruit" (no. 116).

5. In 1518 Luther repeatedly cited as a well-known axiom, *Non sacramentum sed fides sacramenti iustificat*. Discussions of this with Oswald Bayer of Tübingen and Kurt-Victor Selge of Heidelberg helped me to get deeper into Luther's theological shift in 1518 toward emphasis on the objective word of forgiveness.

6. *Luther and His Spiritual Legacy*, 124–25.

designates not a static condition but a process by which *peccatum* comes to be *regnatum* or "ruled sin."[7]

The year 1990 was important in my half-lifetime of study of Luther. That year I got beyond solving problems, whether those caused by myself in the dissertation or by Catholics having a too narrow basis in Luther's texts on *simul iustus et peccator*. I also went beyond the one-sidedly individualistic account of Luther's legacy, which I now realize I had been presenting. One factor may have been my joining in 1986 the world-level Lutheran-Catholic dialogue, on "Justification and the Church," which made it imperative to grasp Luther as a teacher on the church.

A definite occasion that opened new vistas in 1990 was my mentor Iserloh's 75th birthday, for which I lectured in Münster on a constructive theme which I had been researching and over which I was becoming quite enthusiastic. The title was "Holy Spirit – Church – Sanctification: Insights from Luther's Instructions on the Faith," in which I drew extensively from Luther's several catechetical expositions of the Third Article of the Creed.[8] The fact that "sanctification" was in this last title is significant, and it will come back in a moment concerning Law/Gospel.

The aim of my 1990 Münster lecture was to show the constructive positions on the nature and mission of the church that Luther presented in his accounts of the work of the Holy

---

7. The section-headings: The "clothed" God of the Incarnation (pp. 121–23); By the law, conscious awareness of sin (124–25); Remembering Christ (125–26); Passivity (127–29); Laying Hold of Christ by faith (130 –32); The Mediated Promise (132–35); Joyous Certainty (135–37); Exchange with Christ outside myself (137–41); Eruptive Spontaneity in doing good (141–44); Daily expulsion of sin (144–48); Loving Service in Vocation (148–53). But as will become clear just below, that account is incomplete because it focuses one-sidedly on the individual without considering the church, as Luther will do in his catechesis of the Third Article.

8. The Münster lecture for Iserloh came out in German in *Catholica*, the periodical of the Johann-Adam-Moehler Institute in Paderborn, 45 (1991). I was especially happy to have the English text be my first contribution to *Pro Ecclesia*, in vol. 2 (1993). The Luther texts on which it built were the Reformer's account of the Creed, especially the Third Article: (1) in four catechetical sermon-series, once in 1523 and three times in 1528 (WA 11, 48-54 and 30/I, 2-94); (2) in Luther's 1528 confession of faith against Zwingli (WA 26, 499–509; LW 37, 360–72); (3) in the two catechisms of 1529; and in Pentecost sermons of 1529, 1531, and 1538 (WA 29, 359–76; WA 34/I, 458–68; WA 46, 423–33)

Spirit, the Sanctifier. I derived three "theses" from study of Luther's several catechetical texts.

Thesis 1 was general, namely, that when Luther carried out basic Christian instruction, he treated the church within the Holy Spirit's mission of sanctification. The Spirit's mission is the *locus* of ecclesiology, as in the *Large Catechism*.

> God's Spirit alone is called a Holy Spirit, that is, the one who has made us holy and still makes us holy.... The Holy Spirit effects our being made holy through the following: the community (*die Gemeinde*) of saints or Christian church, the forgiveness of sins, the resurrection of the body and life everlasting. That is, he first leads us into his holy community, placing us in the church's lap, where he preaches to us and brings us to Christ.[9]

This work of the Spirit, including the church, has relevance both now and for all time, for every day.

> This, then, is the article that must always remain in force. For creation is now behind us, and redemption has also taken place, but the Holy Spirit continues his work without ceasing until the Last Day, and for this purpose he has appointed a community on earth, through which he speaks and does all his work.[10]

I realize that these are familiar texts to Lutherans, but they fascinated and attracted me immensely when I first studied them and spoke on them in the Auditorium Maximum of Münster on Iserloh's birthday in 1990.

My Thesis 2 arising from Luther's catechetical texts is that the Spirit carries out the work of sanctification not only by assembling believers but as well by richly equipping the ecclesial community with gifts.

---

9. *Large Catechism*, The Creed, nos. 36–37, citing from *The Book of Concord*, eds. Robert Kolb & Timothy Wengert (Minneapolis: Fortress, 2000), 435–36. Also, *Small Catechism*, The Creed, no. 6, where the Holy Spirit's calling and sanctifying "of me" converges with his making holy the whole Christian Church on earth. *Book of Concord*, 355–56.

10. *Large Catechism*, The Creed, no. 61, *Book of Concord*, 439.

The gifts, in Luther's catechesis, are not the Pauline charisms of 1 Cor. 12, but instead the means of grace which mediate sanctification. By them believers are brought to birth and are given forgiveness of sins, that is, by baptism, the sermon, the altar sacrament, absolution, and all the *loci* of consolation.[11] On Pentecost in 1538 Luther contrasted the biblical signs of the Spirit's presence in the past, that is, tongues of fire, the cloud, the dove, with the ecclesial means of grace of today: "The Holy Spirit is the one who outwardly and visibly baptizes and makes use of the word and applies the keys. These are his tongues of fire *(feurig zungen)*."[12]

In Thesis 3, I concluded that the community, gathered and equipped, not only receives sanctification from the Spirit, but as well serves this same Spirit's work, somewhat like an "instrument" of sanctification.

Luther said in a May 1525 catechetical sermon: "What Christ merited by his passion, that the Holy Spirit carries out through his church. Consequently the work of the church is the forgiveness of sins. For she announces the gospel, baptizes, and offers the forgiveness of sins."[13] The church, appointed on earth, is the "executor" through which the Spirit speaks and works.[14] We bear with our weak and sinful flesh here on earth, but still this flesh is being sanctified, by faith and by the church (*per fidem et per ecclesiam*), onward toward eternal life.

Luther wrote concisely in the *Large Catechism* about the holy community of the Christian people: "Through it he [the Holy Spirit] gathers us, using it [the community] to teach and preach the Word. By it he creates and increases holiness, causing it daily to grow and become strong in the faith and in its fruits, which the Spirit produces."[15]

I concluded my account of the Spirit and the church by going over the same texts to draw out what Luther envisioned by

---

11. This, from the December 1528 catechetical sermons, WA 30/I, 92–93.
12. WA 46, 425.
13. WA 30/I, 45.
14. See the text given at note-reference 10, above.
15. *Large Catechism*, The Creed, no. 53; *Book of Concord*, 438.

"sanctification." It has four components: (1) with sanctification beginning with absolution, in virtue of the keys, which imparts forgiveness of sins by God's word of grace. (2) Although sanctification originates *extra nos*, it impacts believers interiorly, enflaming hearts and engendering a sweet and "cordial" relation to God. (3) In sanctification, the Holy Spirit promotes as well new behavior and a different style of life. This is both penitential, in going contrary to sinful flesh, and morally constructive, because one is empowered to observe the commandments. Holiness, Luther once said concisely, is "a person made new, having a different understanding and new morals" (*ut...alium intellectum habeat, novos mores*).[16] The Decalogue plays its role, sketching the profile of the renewed heart and new behavior that the Holy Spirit brings to realization in holiness. (4) Since the whole Third Article is a unity, holiness will come to completion and perfection in resurrection, the Holy Spirit's culminating and wholly complete deed of sanctification.

For me 1990 was a turning point in understanding Luther. My earlier systematization, as in the last 30 pages of *Luther and His Spiritual Legacy,* had highlighted the individual person yearning for the healing grace which moves forward a process of penitential purification, taking the *simul iustus et peccator* not as a static condition but as advancing by God's gifts the "ruled" condition of remaining sin. This is the person growing more integrated — individually — around a disciple's dedication to Christ, to loving service, and more integral worship of the Father.

Luther's catechetical materials bring in a significant new component, with the Holy Spirit looming large as the sanctifier, in whose work Luther spelled out essential roles for the community, through which holiness will grow under the impact of the means of grace — a holiness which the Creed makes us extend its reach to the very end in resurrection unto eternal life. This is, in my reflection, the more comprehensive vision, within which the earlier dramatic process of sin becoming "ruled" in the individual has its place in a broader systematization.

---

16. Sermon, Pentecost Monday, 1528; WA 29, 363

Catholic Reservations Over Law and Gospel

The Lutheran insistence on Law/Gospel does not leave a Catholic theologian cool and reserved because it threatens our consensus on basic truths concerning justification. It is instead a case of reconciled diversity, which remains diverse, as the JDDJ states in section 4.5, nos. 31–33. The Declaration, in no. 32, also gives us Catholics a concise account of the religious or spiritual impact of Law/Gospel.

> In its theological use, the law is demand and accusation. Throughout their lives, all persons, Christians also, in that they are sinners, stand under this accusation which uncovers their sin so that, in faith in the gospel, they turn unreservedly to the mercy of God in Christ, which alone justifies them.

Last May, at a meeting of the current round of our USA dialogue, Timothy Wengert drew on Melanchthon's *Apology*, on CA XII, to explain how this teaching offers the greatest consolation, when it is applied rightly, that is, to "the struggle of the terrified conscience."

> We say that contrition is the genuine terror of the conscience that feels God's wrath against sin and grieves that it has sinned. This contrition takes place when the Word of God denounces sin, because the sum of the preaching of the gospel is to condemn sin and to offer the forgiveness of sins, righteousness on account of Christ, the Holy Spirit, and eternal life, so that having been reborn we might do good.[17]

---

17. *Apology*, XII, no. 29, citing *Book of Concord*, 191–92, given by T. Wengert, on p. 7 of "The Hermeneutic for Reading Scripture as Reflected in the Augsburg Confession," unpublished paper presented May 25, 2012, at the second meeting of Round XII of the US Lutheran – Roman Catholic Dialogue. At the same meeting, Ian McFarland of Emory University presented "Law and Gospel in Lutheran Biblical Hermeneutics and Theology." He emphasized that Luther took Law/Gospel as a way, coming from Scripture, to meet the age-old problem of how the Jewish Scriptures are integral to Christian Scripture. Luther saw the economy of salvation attested in the whole canon in which the one Word of God is differentiated by the interrelated functions of command and promise. These are all through Scripture and they constantly claim the believer's attention to their revelation of human inability and God's free forgiveness.

Beyond these helpful clarifications, our Catholic reluctance begins when we hear about the debates over the law, first at the time of the *Formula of Concord*. Then in the 20th century, several Lutheran theologians responded to Karl Barth but did not agree with each other, especially over the nature and role of law in the ongoing life of a person justified by the grace of the gospel.[18] This leaves the impression that a non-Lutheran theologian has to work through some complicated battlefield theologies if he or she is "get" Law/Gospel correctly in the 21st century.

A further Catholic response, pondering Melanchthon's striking account of the phases of terror in the conscience and the assurance and comfort of the gospel, has to acknowledge a certain similarity with the opening meditations of the Ignatian *Spiritual Exercises*, with which I began this paper. Also, taking the move as a daily spiritual clarification under God's differentiated Word, recalls the spiritual axiom of *semper a novo incipere*, that is, of always, daily, beginning anew from the foundational message of God's Word.

In the tradition from Bernard of Clairvaux, this maxim had an expanded form, "*Proficere est nihil aliud nisi semper a novo incipere*" ("To move ahead is nothing else but to always begin anew").[19] I take Law/Gospel as inculcating this, but Lutheran thought and life leave the impression that this principle gets isolated from other concerns given us in Scripture and its sound teaching on Christian living. *The New Westminster Dictionary of Christian Spirituality* (2005) has entries, which draw on Scripture and the great tradition, in order to present topics like "Ascent," or the "Spiritual Journey," or "Spiritual Growth," with each pointing to life

---

18. In the paper mentioned in the previous note, McFarland surveyed, "Law and Gospel in the Modern Period," treating the Luther Renaissance, Karl Barth and Barmen, Werner Elert, Paul Althaus, several Missouri Synod interpreters, and David Yeago, before he concluded on Law/Gospel in its significance for explaining Scripture's essential unity.

19. In Luther's first lectures on the Psalms, I found Luther treating spiritual progress as always beginning anew. See *Man Yearning for Grace*, 88–90. On the impact of St. Bernard of Clairvaux on Luther, we now have Franz Posset's *The Real Luther. A Friar at Erfurt and Wittenberg. Exploring Luther's Life with Melanchthon as Guide* (St. Louis: Concordia Publishing House, 2012), especially pp. 85–128.

unfolding beyond the foundational passage from the terrified conscience to the comfort of forgiveness because of Christ. Catholic theology wants to serve these concerns regarding the further development of the person in the new life graciously given.

My own approach to this issue is to take up Luther's account of sanctification as I found this in his accounts of the Creed's Third Article. This is to set ecclesiology within the Spirit's sanctifying mission, giving to the church and our spiritual lives a well-rounded trinitarian framework. The means of grace figure importantly here, so that the notion of holiness is well anchored — kept free of dominance by philosophies of the person, whether Platonic, Aristotelian, neo-Platonic, existentialist, or self-constructionalist. Holiness, so conceived, looks to seeing things differently and living in accord with this vision (*alium intellectum ...novos mores*), which indicates pathways of spiritual growth and personal flourishing — moving on under the grace given by the comforting gospel. I want to keep insisting on this precious instruction by Luther on sanctification, in the hope that by it he can continue speaking to us all for our personal and ministerial flourishing.

Did Luther Get Paul Right on Justification?

Stephen Westerholm

If you ask, "Did Luther get Paul right on justification?" it will be because you know there are people who think he did not. That has been true from the very beginning, of course, but it has lately become almost the standard view among Pauline scholars, and it is this particular challenge that I intend to focus on in this paper.[1] We may take the opening words of Galatians 2:16 as our starting-point: "Knowing that a person is not justified by works of the law, but through faith in Jesus Christ." Now Luther certainly thought justification was about how sinners might find a gracious God. But ever since a famous article by Krister Stendahl in the early 1960s,[2] many Pauline scholars have denied that that was even an issue for the apostle; his concern was with the terms by which non-Jews could be admitted to the people of God. Luther thought Paul meant that a person can be justified only by grace, not by anything he/she does. With E. P. Sanders, many scholars deny that that *could* have been Paul's point, since, in their view, there was nothing controversial about it; they claim that non-Christian Jews no less than

---

1. This paper was prepared for oral presentation at the conference, "Preaching and Teaching the Law and Gospel of God," held in Golden Valley, Minnesota, August 15-16, 2012. I have retained the oral style of the presentation, adding only a few footnotes by way of documentation. For fuller argumentation and documentation, see my *Perspectives Old and New on Paul: The "Lutheran" Paul and His Critics* (Grand Rapids: Eerdmans, 2004); or (more concisely) *Understanding Paul: The Early Christian Worldview of the Letter to the Romans* (2nd edition; Grand Rapids: Baker Academic, 2004); "The Righteousness of the Law and the Righteousness of Faith" (*Interpretation* 58 [2004], 253-264).
2. "The Apostle Paul and the Introspective Conscience of the West." *Harvard Theological Review* 56 (1963), 199-215; reproduced in Krister Stendahl, *Paul Among Jews and Gentiles and Other Essays* (Philadelphia: Fortress Press, 1976), 78-96.

Paul believed that salvation is by grace.³ Luther thought that when Paul talked about how we are "justified," he meant how we are declared righteous by God rather than condemned as sinners; with Tom Wright, many scholars today think he was talking about who belonged to God's family, who had the right to sit at table with the people of God.⁴ Luther thought that, when Paul denies that we can be justified by works of the law, he meant that people cannot be justified by the good things they do. With Jimmy Dunn, many scholars today think he was denying that particular works demanded by the law — namely, circumcision, Sabbath observance, and Jewish food laws — were required of Gentile believers.⁵

So here is the problem in a nutshell: when Paul writes, "A person is not justified by works of the law, but by faith in Jesus Christ," does he mean, "Sinners cannot stand as approved before God on the basis of good things they do, but only by grace, through faith in Jesus Christ"? That is Luther's position, for our purposes. Or does he mean, "Gentiles are not required to get circumcised and keep other distinctively Jewish practices to be given a place among the people of God"? That is the position of many Pauline scholars today. I am going to argue that, in this debate, Luther got Paul right. But let me set the stage by pointing out why the alternative seems plausible to many scholars today.

The earliest followers of Jesus were all Jews. If you read the Gospels, you do not get the idea that Jesus' followers were among the Jews who were most punctilious about observing the law. That is undoubtedly true, but it does not mean that their males were not circumcised. Perhaps they were not as careful as some about the fine points of Sabbath observance (cf. Mark 2:23-28); still, it would not have occurred even to the earliest followers of Jesus to go about their ordinary business on the day of

---

3. E. P. Sanders, *Paul and Palestinian Judaism: A Comparison of Patterns of Religion* (Philadelphia: Fortress Press, 1977), p. 543.

4. N. T. Wright, *Justification: God's Plan and Paul's Vision* (Downers Grove, IL: IVP Academic, 2009), p. 116.

5. James D. G. Dunn, "The New Perspective on Paul: whence, what, and whither?" (pages 1-88 in Dunn's *The New Perspective on Paul: Collected Essays* [Grand Rapids: Eerdmans Publishing Co., 2005]), pp. 22-26.

rest. Ceremonial handwashing before eating was probably not their forte (cf. Mark 7:1-23); but you can be sure pork chops were never on their menu. Peter, you may remember, was pretty sure he should not be a guest of Gentile Cornelius until he was given explicit instructions otherwise (Acts 10:9-28). Besides, most of the early Christians were not thinkers like Paul. They had always kept the law, more or less; and after Christ's resurrection, they simply went on, "more or less" keeping the law. The question whether followers of Christ *should* or *should not* be doing so probably did not even arise in their minds — until Gentile converts showed up at their doorstep. Gentile *sinners*, that is, uncircumcised, Sabbath-breaking, pig-eating Gentiles. What in the world were they to do now?

Some people were clear enough on the matter. And give them credit. They believed in Jesus as Messiah, in his atoning death, glorious resurrection, and exaltation on high. But in their minds, God's chosen people were still the Jews; the law of Moses was still the law of God. Messiah had come, to be sure, but he came in fulfillment of *Jewish* hopes: in these people's minds, his coming did nothing to alter the constitution or covenant of the chosen people of God. Gentiles were welcome, to be sure, but they had to become Jews. "Start with circumcision," they told them. Such, presumably, was the line taken by conservative Jewish believers at the Apostolic Council described in Acts 15. It was the position of Paul's opponents in Galatia. These were the hardliners — though it must be admitted that there is a certain plausibility about their stance.

Then there were the fence-sitters, Jewish believers with no clear convictions one way or the other, liable to be moved *either* way with the prevailing wind. Surprising as it may sound, it appears that Peter was among their number. When he first visited the community of believers in Antioch, he was impressed by the unity on display as Gentile and Jewish believers ate at the same table. He sat down and ate with them. Then messengers from James in Jerusalem arrived and told him, "Stop doing that!" Peter got up and left the table (Gal. 2:11-12). Such vacillating surely suggests that Peter's own mind was less than clear on the issue. Of course, that was when Paul stood up and accused Peter of hypocrisy (2:13-14). It would be nice to know how Peter responded. We do not know, but it is precisely at this point that Paul first formulates the principle, "A person is not justified by works of the law, but by faith in Jesus Christ" (2:16). Should we not conclude that the words were suited to the occasion? That Paul was saying, in effect, Gentiles do not need to be circumcised and keep other Jewish practices to sit at table with Jewish believers? That, after all, is what was at stake in Antioch — not whether sinners can be found righteous by the good things they do.

> So the argument goes. Let Tom Wright sum it up. Elsewhere
>
> "justified" was a law court term meaning "given the status of being 'in the right.'" But [in Gal. 2:11-16] Paul is not in a law court, he is at a dinner table. The context of his talking about "not being justified by works of the law" is that he is confronted with the question of ethnic taboos about eating together across ethnic boundaries.... We are forced to conclude, at least in a preliminary way, that "to be justified" here does not mean "to be granted free forgiveness of your sins," "to come into a right relation with God" or some other near-synonym of "to be reckoned 'in the right' before God," but rather, and very specifically, "to be reckoned by God to be a true member of his family, and hence with the right to share table fellowship."[6]

It makes, one must admit, some sense in this context; but there is something "fishy," is there not, about treating "justified" as though it meant "entitled to share table fellowship"? Can the word really mean that? So we wonder, and the only way to ease our troubled minds is with a little word study.

At issue, in the first place, are the Hebrew adjective *tzaddiq*, "righteous," the noun *tzedeqah*, "righteousness," and the verb in the hiphil stem, *hitzdiq*, which is normally translated "justify," but which I will render "find" or "declare righteous" in order to underline its relation with the adjective and noun. These terms

---

6. Wright, *Justification*, p. 116.

are typically rendered *dikaios, dikaiosyne,* and *dikaioo* in the Greek version of the Old Testament, and Paul clearly uses the Greek terms without meaning anything different from their Hebrew equivalents. The first, most fundamental thing to be said about these terms is that they belong to the basic moral vocabulary of the Hebrew and Greek languages. "Righteousness" is an abstract term for what one is morally obligated to do. And the "righteous" person is the person who does "righteousness," who does what one *ought* to do. In the Hebrew Scriptures, the *tzaddiq* is more or less synonymous with the "blameless" (Gen. 6:9; Job 12:4), the "innocent" (Job 22:19; Ps 94:21), the "upright in heart" (Ps. 32:11; 97:11). The opposite of being "righteous" is being "wicked." It is, of course, important to add that, given the distortion of our moral compass caused by sin, different people may have somewhat different understandings of what is the right thing to do. It is also true that people with different world views will have different understandings of what *makes* certain things the right things to do, and what *makes* other things the wrong things to do. But for the moment my point is simply that when Ezekiel describes the righteous person in Ezekiel 18, he means the person who does what he ought to do. And when the First Epistle of John tells us that it is the one who does righteousness who is righteous (3:7), the simple point is that it is the person who does what he ought to do who is righteous.

A couple illustrations. For the first one, we return to Ezekiel 18. There Ezekiel describes the *tzaddiq*, the righteous man, as one who "does not eat on the mountains, or lift up his eyes to the idols of the house of Israel, or defile his neighbor's wife, or approach a woman ceremonially unclean; does not oppress anyone, but gives back to the debtor his pledge; commits no robbery, gives his bread to the hungry, covers the naked with clothing, does not lend at interest or take interest," and so on (Ezek. 18:5-9). Two things should be perfectly clear: first, Ezekiel means, by the righteous person, the one who does what he ought to do; second, Ezekiel's notion of what one ought to do overlaps but does not completely coincide with the notions of most people today. When Proverbs tells us that the righteous person is concerned about the well-being of the poor (29:7) and of animals (12:10), hates lying (13:5), and shows generosity (21:26), we might think that its ideas are no different from the way people think today. But that misleading impression only lasts until we realize that Proverbs thinks the righteous person is the same as the wise person, and that the righteous or wise person gets on well in this world, has a full stomach, a full barn, good health, and long life, whereas the wicked person is doomed to earthly trouble (e.g., 10:3, 24, 27; 11:8, 31; 12:21; 13:25). When we read these latter texts, we are reminded that, in spite of some similarities, in the end Proverbs sees the world very differently from the way most people do today.

For Proverbs, as for all the writers of Hebrew Scripture and for Paul as well, we live in a world ordered by the wisdom of God. If the world is ordered by the wisdom of God, then the *right* thing to do is also the wise thing to do: namely, to refrain from doing what is wise or right *in our own eyes* (Prov. 3:7; 12:15; 16:2; 21:2; 30:12), and to seek out that course of action that is in harmony with the divine wisdom that formed the world in the beginning and sustains it to this day (3:19; 8:12-36). Naturally, Proverbs expects that those who live in harmony with the order of the cosmos will get on well within it. And even if they do not, it is still better, says Proverbs, it is more in keeping with the wisdom that runs the world, to be poor and maintain one's integrity than rich and crooked in one's dealings (28:6; cf. 19:22). To do what is right is to be righteous and wise. And it all begins with the fear of the Lord (1:7).

As the divine order according to which we ought to live pervades the whole universe, so expectations of right behavior are universal. It is important to emphasize that the language of righteousness and wickedness in the Hebrew Scriptures is by no means confined to the covenant people of God. No book in Scripture has more to say about the righteous and the wicked than Proverbs. But the vision of Proverbs, as of wisdom literature in general, is universal; it is certainly not confined to the people of one nation or covenant. Nothing prevents a non-Israelite from being found "righteous" in the Hebrew Scriptures. Noah made the grade (Gen. 6:9; 7:1; cf. 20:4), and there was nothing in principle unreasonable in the expectation that in a Canaanite city the size of Sodom, at least fifty *tzaddiqim*, fifty righteous people, could be found (Gen. 18:24). Abraham was sure there would be, though to be on the safe side he asked God to spare the city even if the number was cut to ten. Here is the point: the Canaanite people of Sodom did not belong to the covenant people of God, but they were still expected to be righteous. And Sodom was destroyed because its people were *not* righteous. The oracles against the nations delivered by Old Testament prophets presuppose the obligation of people everywhere to do what is right, and their liability to judgment when they do not. Human beings *as human beings* are moral beings. To be human is to be responsible before God to be righteous, to do what one ought.

Did people have to be perfect to be considered righteous? Generally speaking, no. Among the marks of those who live as they ought to live in Proverbs is their willingness to listen to rebuke (12:1; 13:18; 15:5). One needs rebuke when one has *not* acted as one should. So these people are considered righteous because their basic orientation is to do what is right, not because they always do so. They are willing to learn, and to abide by what they learn. On the other hand, there are a few Old Testament texts that use the language of righteousness in a stricter sense. One of them is alluded to by Paul: Psalm 143:2: "Do not enter into judgment with your servant; for no one living is righteous before you." Or Job 15:14: "What is man, that he can be clean? What is he that is born of a woman, that he can be righteous?" The point then is that, strictly speaking, no human being can be righteous before God; so great is the gap between human beings and God that the term "righteous" cannot be used in the same sense of both (cf. also Job 4:17; 25:4-6). That is certainly a point worth making, but the texts that make it are few. Most Old Testament texts are content to ascribe righteousness to imperfect human beings who are rightly oriented toward God and seek to do his commands.

So that is what righteousness is, and who the righteous are. What about the verb, "declare righteous"? It is used most commonly in legal or legal-type situations where a judge decides who is in the right. Note that, while what is being judged is not one's overall character as righteous or sinner, but only whether one is in the right in the specific incident under review, the judge's verdict nonetheless pertains precisely to whether one is in the right, whether one has acted as one ought, in that particular instance. Ethical behavior is still the issue. Note, too, that the verdict of the judge is not what *makes* a person righteous or wicked. The righteous person is the person who has done what is right, whether or not judges recognize their righteousness. Naboth was falsely accused and condemned at the instigation of Jezebel (1 Kgs. 21:1-14); that he was condemned by judges did not change the fact that he was innocent, or righteous; he remained righteous in spite of his condemnation because he had not committed the wrongful act for which he was condemned. Conversely, the sinner, the guilty party, is the person who actually did what is wrong, whether or not a judge pronounces him guilty. A murderer does not become righteous when a corrupt judge accepts a bribe and acquits him of the charge of murder. Human courts get it right sometimes, but they can also get it wrong. Warnings against declaring righteous the guilty, or declaring guilty the righteous (cf. Exod. 23:7; Deut. 25:1; Isa. 5:23), make clear that whether or not one is righteous depends on what one has or has not done, regardless of the judges' decision in the matter. To repeat: neither righteousness nor its opposite, wickedness, is a status conveyed by a judge's decision. Both are rather the result of the kind of person one is, and the nature of one's own actions.

All this seems smashingly self-evident, so what is the point? Just this: nothing in the Old Testament usage of the terms supports the claim of our Pauline revisionists that, when Paul talks about how a person is "justified," he means how people find themselves part of the family, or part of the covenant, or entitled to sit at the family table. That is simply not what the term means. You *can* be righteous inside a covenant, but you can *also* be righteous outside any covenant. Conversely, the Israelites who entered a covenant with God at Mount Sinai then found themselves wandering in the wilderness for forty years because they were stubborn and stiff-necked, not "righteous" (Deut. 9:4-7). To be righteous is to be the kind of person one ought to be, to have done what one ought to do. To "justify," to "declare righteous," is to declare that someone has done as they ought.

Now Paul has some striking things to say about righteousness and justification. But he does not change the meaning of the words when he says them; if he had done that, no one would have known what he was talking about. I have said that the language of righteousness is basic ethical vocabulary in Hebrew and Greek; the same is true in Paul. For Paul, too, righteousness denotes what one ought to do, the equivalent of the good, the opposite of sin. When Romans 6 contrasts a life lived in the service of sin with a life in service of righteousness, it is clear that, whatever else we may say about the terms, "righteousness" is what one ought to do, and "sin" what one should not. The same is true when Paul insists that a believer should not be mismated with an unbeliever because righteousness and iniquity have nothing in common with each other (2 Cor. 6:14). When Paul, quoting the Psalms, says in Romans 3:10 that there is none righteous, he goes on to demonstrate people's *un*righteousness by providing a list of things that they should *not* do but do anyway, and of things they *ought* to do but do not (3:10-18).

Furthermore, for Paul, the verb *dikaioo*, like the Hebrew verb *hitzdiq*, means "declare righteous," "find righteous," "acquit." Paul tells the Corinthians that he is not aware of having done them any wrong, but then he admits that that does not mean he is off the hook; after all, he cannot declare *himself* righteous. Only God, who knows the heart, can do that (1 Cor. 4:1-5). The assessment of moral behavior is the issue, not table fellowship. According to Romans 2, it is not the hearers of the law who are righteous before God, but the doers of the law who will be *found righteous* (Rom. 2:13). These and other passages prove that Paul, too, uses righteousness language in its ordinary, moral sense.

And for the apostle, too, the obligation to do what is right is universal, because human beings are moral beings living in a world ordered by the wisdom of God. In such a universe, it is only wise and appropriate and right for human beings to recognize and acknowledge their dependence on their Creator, to give him worship and thanks (Rom.1:19-21); their failure to do so — and Paul indicates that the failure is universal — is the fundamental human sin, though it naturally finds expression in other violations of the wise ordering of God's creation. Refuse to acknowledge the Creator and you are not likely to acknowledge the created order either, and Paul goes on in Romans 1 to illustrate various ways in which sinful human beings, who have suppressed the truth about God, now live "contrary to nature" as well (1:26-27): contrary, that is, to what is appropriate in, and in conformity with, the natural order as created by God. Against such ungodliness and wickedness the wrath of God is even now poured out (1:18), though this does not preclude a final revelation of divine judgment at the end of time (2:5-6). All of this is important, but for the moment the point I want to emphasize is that for Paul, as for all the writers of Scripture, God's requirement of righteous behavior pertains to *all* human beings. That these expectations are not met is precisely the basis for the "wrath to come" of which Paul also speaks (1 Thess. 1:10; 5:3).

Having denounced universal human unrighteousness in Romans 1 without reference to the law God gave to Israel, Paul develops his argument in Romans 2 by showing the relationship between God's universal expectations of righteousness and the commands given in the law of Moses. What he says is essential, though often overlooked. After insisting that God is going to judge all human beings, without partiality, according to their works, rewarding those who have done what is good, punishing those who have done what is evil (2:6-11), Paul goes on to indicate that the law spells out the content of the good that God expects all human beings to do. Clearly, he is thinking of the *moral* demands of Mosaic law. Even Gentiles have some awareness of these requirements, Paul writes, because God has written them on their hearts. How do we know that Gentiles are aware of God's moral requirements? How do we know that God has written them on human hearts? Gentiles *show* their awareness of what they ought to do whenever they actually do it (2:14-15). Note that Paul is not at this point talking about Gentile Christians; still less is he saying that there are Gentile *non*-Christians who consistently do what is right and who therefore will be found righteous on the day of judgment. He merely claims that at times even Gentiles do the right thing; and when they do, they show their awareness of their moral obligations, obligations that bind Gentiles no less than they bind Jews. The only difference in this regard is that God has spelled out human moral obligations for the benefit of Jews in the Mosaic law. As a result, Jews are able to teach Gentiles about their mutual responsibilities. The Jew who is instructed in the law is in a position to be a guide to the blind, a light to those in darkness, a corrector of the foolish — in each case by instructing Gentiles in the moral obligations incumbent upon them both: you shall not steal, you shall not commit adultery, and so on (2:17-22).

And God, Paul says, will judge Jew and Gentile alike as to whether or not they have actually fulfilled these demands: whether or not they have done what is good (2:7-10), or — in an equivalent expression — whether or not they are doers of the law (2:13). God's judgment is impartial, and makes no mistakes: it is the doers of the laws who are righteous, and God will declare them so (2:11, 13). Whether a person is righteous or wicked depends on whether they do what is good or what is evil, whether they are doers of the law or its transgressors. And God, who knows all about them, will reward them accordingly.

Let me sum up what we have seen so far. Revisionist scholars these days say that when Paul talks about justification, he is talking about who is a member of the covenant, about whether Gentile believers need to keep Jewish practices if they are to belong to God's people and sit at their table. Well, certainly relations between Gentile and Jewish believers were a concern for Paul; but that is not the point of his language of righteousness, or justification. Righteousness is what human beings ought to do, and God will judge people by whether or not they are righteous, whether or not they have done what is right. The righteousness that human beings ought to do is something that all human beings have some awareness of because God has written it on their hearts; but it is also something that God has spelled out in the moral commandments of the Mosaic law. Thus God will find righteous those who do what is right, those who are doers of the law. When Paul talks about a righteousness based on law, he is talking about a righteousness acquired by fulfilling the righteous demands of the law; ultimately it is a righteousness required no less of Gentiles than of Jews.

Paul speaks further of the righteousness based on law in later chapters in Romans as well as in Galatians and Philippians. It would certainly be worth our while to go through each reference carefully, but for our purposes I must confine myself to a couple of general observations.

First: Paul finds the fundamental principle of the righteousness based on law in Leviticus 18:5, a text he quotes both in Romans 10:5 and in Galatians 3:12: "The one who does these things [i.e., the one who does what the law commands] will live by them." Note that this in perfect agreement with what we have seen in Romans 2:13: it is the doers of the law who will be found righteous. The law, by its very nature, requires observance of its commands. And the righteousness of the law is acquired by such observance.

Second: if the law by its very nature requires deeds, or works, as its condition for blessing, then it is clear that a righteousness based on the law and a righteousness based on *works of the law* are two different ways of saying the same thing. The latter phrase occurs in both Galatians and Romans; and in both Galatians and Romans it is interchangeable with the shorter expression: righteousness based on "works of the law" is the same as righteousness based on "law" (compare Gal. 2:16 with 2:21 and 5:4; compare Rom. 3:20, 28 with 3:21 and 10:5). It is thus a distortion of Paul's point to say that, when Paul insists that "a person is not justified by works of the law" in Galatians and Romans, he is merely concerned with whether or not Gentile believers should observe a few particular "works of the law," such as circumcision, Sabbath, and the food laws. To be sure, that was the question facing the Galatians to whom Paul wrote;

but he addresses the question by raising the more fundamental issue of whether anyone, Jew or Gentile, can be righteous before God by doing what the law requires. Those who know that the law is simply not viable as a path to righteousness will not be tempted to take on the observance of the boundary markers it prescribes.

On two crucial points, then, Luther is right, and his modern critics are wrong: to be "justified," "declared righteous," does *not* mean declared to be within the covenant, entitled to sit at the family table. It means "declared righteous," "found innocent," acquitted of any charge of wrongdoing. And when Paul says people are not justified by "works of the law," he is not talking about a few Jewish practices, but about the righteous behavior prescribed by the law and expected of Gentiles as well; it amounts to the same thing as the "doing good" of Romans 2:7, 10, or what is otherwise referred to as "good works."

But here is the problem: if the law was given by God, and meant to be obeyed; and if those who obey the law are righteous, how can Paul say that righteousness cannot come by the law? What *is* his point in saying that "a person is not justified by works of the law, but through faith in Jesus Christ"?

Paul addresses the issue primarily in Galatians and Romans, but for the moment I want to begin with 2 Corinthians 3. The glory of the old covenant, centered in the law carved in letters on stone, has been surpassed by the glory of the new covenant; but there *was* divine glory, even with the old covenant; it, too, was given by God. And yet its service was a service characterized by "death," Paul writes in verse 7; by "condemnation," he writes in verse 9. The latter term is the revealing one. The law "condemns" those who transgress it. In principle, of course, the law promises both blessing and life to those who obey its commands *and* cursing and death to those who disobey (Deut. 30:15-20). But when Paul says that the service of the law is simply one of condemnation and never even mentions the law's promise of blessing for those who obey it, it must be because he thinks there is nobody who does, in fact, obey the law; the law's commands have universally been broken, so that the only practical effect of the law has been condemnation.

That is the story, as Paul sees it, in a nutshell. It is the same story in Galatians and Romans, though in these letters Paul develops the point at greater length. In Galatians, "all who are dependent on works of the law are under a curse" (Gal. 3:10). Again, the law's promise of blessing for those who obey its commands is not even mentioned as a possibility. If we ask why not, the obvious answer is that the law has not been obeyed: the law curses "everyone who does not abide by all things written in the book of the law, to do them" (Gal. 3:10, referring to Deut. 27:26). When Romans 3:19-20 concludes that no human being will be found righteous in God's sight by works of the law, the conclusion is based on the argument found in Romans 1:18-3:20. Here, even though the principle of the law is repeated — "the doers of the law will be found righteous" (2:13) — Paul insists, and he quotes Scripture to support his point, that no one is righteous, no one does what is right (3:9-20). Gentiles suppress their knowledge of God and fail to give him the honor he is due; and though they know that those who do wrong deserve to die, they do it anyway (1:18, 21, 32). Jews boast of their knowledge of God's will because they are instructed in the law, but they themselves break the laws that they are eager to teach others (2:1-24). All have sinned and come short of God's glory (3:23), and therefore none can be righteous by "works of the law": by doing what they ought to do and what the law demands.

Paul claims that all have sinned, that all transgress the law, and therefore that no one can be righteous by works of the law. But as the argument of Romans continues, it becomes clear that the human dilemma goes even deeper. It is not only the case that all human beings commit sin. All, Gentiles and Jews alike, are "under the power of sin" (Rom.3:9). In Adam they have *become sinners*, and live in a realm over which sin reigns (Rom. 5). They are slaves of sin (Rom .6). They live in a flesh in which there is no good thing (Rom. 7). The whole mindset of the flesh is hostile to God, does not submit to God's law, and cannot please God (Rom. 8:7-8). In short, human beings choose to commit sins, and they are also the captives of sin; they both embrace sin and are entangled in sin. Hence not only is it the case that their actual sins prevent them from being found righteous. Such righteousness is totally out of their reach. The law, though holy and just and good in all its demands (7:12), is too weak to secure its fulfillment from sinful flesh (8:3).

Time again for a summing up. Paul shared with his fellow Jews the conviction, first, that the cosmos is ordered by God; second, that in principle the righteous are those who live in conformity with the wisdom of the created order; third, that God has given Jews the law of Moses spelling out the righteousness he requires, so that the doers of the law will be found righteous. Where he differs dramatically from his fellow Jews is in his belief that the circle of those who will be found righteous in this ordinary sense of the word, because they have done what is right, because they have done what they ought: the circle of the righteous has no one inside it. The problem, of course, is not with the law, or even with Jewish interpretations of the law's demands; and it is certainly not with God's requirement that people do what they ought to do. The problem is that human beings have chosen to do otherwise, and are now incapable of reversing their direction.

Why is Paul so much more pessimistic about the human capacity to do good than other Jews? In my mind, there is no mystery here. Paul had come to see that the divine remedy for human sinfulness was the crucifixion of the Messiah. So catastrophic a remedy implies a catastrophic predicament. After all, if righteousness were attainable under the law, then there was no reason for Christ to die (Gal. 2:21). But Christ had died. So righteousness is not attainable under the law. Why not? The problem cannot be a failure on God's part. It can only mean that human beings have not fulfilled God's commands. Thus the radical nature of human *un*righteousness and *un*godliness is only apparent in the light of the cross. The cross of Christ reveals the depths of human sinfulness at the same time as it reveals the depths of divine love.

This means that Paul's dire depiction of the human dilemma is in fact only the backdrop for his proclamation of the divine solution. Paul was no pessimist by nature, nor could he be a pessimist as an apostle of Jesus Christ. If human beings prove, individually and *en masse*, to be *un*righteous; if righteousness in the ordinary sense of the word proves impossible for human beings because they do not do what they ought, then God will open to them the possibility of an extraordinary righteousness. If sinful human beings fall short of the righteousness of the law, God will make available to them the righteousness of faith. To that righteousness we will turn shortly.

But perhaps the question should first be asked why God bothered to give a law if he knew people were not going to obey it anyway. The question *is* often asked, though, to my mind, it appears to make sense only as long as we keep it at a general level; as soon as we ask it of specific commands in the law, its foolishness becomes evident. Why did God tell people not to murder if he knew that people would murder anyway? Why did God tell people not to commit adultery if he knew they were going to commit adultery anyway? Why did God tell people not to steal if he knew they were going to steal anyway? Why? Because, whether nobody commits murder, adultery, or theft, or whether *everyone* does so makes no difference whatsoever to the moral obligation, binding on all human beings, not to commit murder, adultery, or theft. We can go a step further. Paul tells us that the commandments of the law are righteous and good (Rom. 7:12). He tells us that sin was in the world before the law was given (Rom. 5:13). Murder, adultery, and theft did not *become* wrong when God gave the ten commandments to Moses. In a cosmos made and sustained by the wise order of the Creator, murder, adultery, and theft are inherently wrong, have always been wrong, and always will be wrong. The giving of the law simply spelled out in unmistakable terms the moral obligations incumbent on all who would live in God's universe. (And, incidentally, there is nowhere else to live.)

That means that the righteousness of the law is part of the fabric of the universe in which we live. When God made human beings in his image, he made beings with a moral sense and moral responsibilities. To be human is to be obligated to do good, to avoid evil; put differently, to be human is to be obligated to fulfill the moral demands of the law. But we are not the human beings we were made to be. Therefore the righteousness of the law is beyond our reach. To remind us of our moral responsibilities, and to make evident our moral failures, God spelled out those responsibilities in the law of Moses. But if sinful human beings are to be righteous, something other than the righteousness of the law is required. So far, Paul; and — it would be fair to add — so far, Luther. And we may take one step further: the problem arising out of what Paul says about righteousness can be summed up in the simple question: How can I find a gracious God?

If the righteousness of the law were the only story, God's creation would end in failure; but that, of course, is inconceivable. The very cross of Christ that reveals the depths of human sinfulness is also the means by which God puts things right in his creation. Immediately after concluding that no flesh will be declared righteous in God's sight by works of the law (Rom. 3:20), Paul announces the revelation of God's righteousness based on faith: "But now the righteousness of God has been manifested apart from law, the righteousness of God through faith in Jesus Christ for all who believe" (Rom. 3:21-22). On this righteousness, I want to make seven points — briefly!

First, that righteousness is based on faith rather than on works of the law does not mean that God has simply lowered the standard, so that he now requires no more than what humans themselves are capable of. Paul does not think of faith as a human work at all; on the contrary, he repeatedly contrasts faith and works (Rom. 4:4-5; 9:32; Gal. 3:11-12). To be sure, faith marks the community of the redeemed, who can simply be referred to as "the believing ones," *hoi pisteuontes* (1 Cor. 14:22; 1 Thess. 1:7; 2:10, 13). Those outside the community are *hoi apistoi*, "unbelievers" (1 Cor. 6:6; 10:27; 14:22-24). So Paul can speak of what distinguishes those being saved from those who are perishing as the faith of the former (1 Cor. 1:21). But such faith is never a quality inherent in the individual who believes. Faith, the faith of the believer, is a response called into being by the proclamation of the gospel ("faith comes from what is heard, and the message is heard through the preaching of Christ" [Rom. 10:17]); alternatively, Paul can say that what is heard in the proclamation of the gospel is the *call* of God (2 Thess. 2:14), so that "believers" in one verse can be identified as "the called ones" in another (compare 1 Cor. 1:21 and 24). The word of God is said to be "active" in those who believe (1 Thess. 2:13), so that their faith can itself be spoken of as a gift from God (Phil. 1:29). A response of faith to the gospel is critical to justification, but that is not to say that sinners initiate the process by deciding to believe. It is merely to recognize that God's free gift of righteousness must be received if it is to be enjoyed; and God creates the possibility of its reception.

Second: those who believe are righteous "by God's grace as a gift" (3:24) — and necessarily so, for obviously the *un*righteous have no claim of their own to be righteous. Romans 5:17 again links together "grace and the free gift of righteousness." In Philippians 3:9, too, the righteousness of faith is a gift "from God." So those who believe receive righteousness as a free gift of God's grace. Conversely, though no one in fact is righteous by doing what the law requires, in principle, if people *were* righteous in the ordinary sense of the word (by doing what is right), their righteousness *would* be to their credit, not a gift of grace: "to one who works, his wages are not reckoned as a gift but as his due" (Rom. 4:4). Later on in Romans 4, Paul says that God's promise of an inheritance to Abraham depended on faith precisely in order that it might "rest on grace" (4:16). Had Abraham received the inheritance because he observed the law, he would not have received it on the basis of grace. Ephesians 2:8-9 sums up the linkage between grace and faith perfectly: "For by grace you have been saved through faith; and this is not your own doing, it is the gift of God — not because of works, lest anyone should boast."

Third: that God is gracious in declaring the unrighteous righteous is clear enough; but is it right for him to do so? Paul himself raises the issue in Romans 3:25-26, but it is also implicitly present when he says that God "declares righteous the ungodly" in Romans 4:5. The Greek word translated "ungodly" is the same word used in the Greek version of Old Testament texts (Exod. 23:7; Deut. 25:1; Isa 5:23) where judges are told that they are to declare righteous those who are righteous, and emphatically *not* to declare righteous the ungodly. Judges who acquit, who declare the ungodly righteous, are corrupt judges, rendering unjust judgment in return for a bribe. But such unjust judgment — acquitting the ungodly, declaring innocent the guilty, declaring righteous the unrighteous — is apparently what God has done, according to Romans 4:5. Obviously, such judgment, when God is the judge, can hardly be in return for a bribe; God cannot be considered a corrupt judge in that sense. But is he *just*? The same question is raised by Romans 5:8-9, where Paul again speaks of God declaring sinners righteous: how can *that* be right?

God can be both just *and* the justifier of the one who believes in Jesus, he can be both righteous and the one who declares sinners righteous, because he has put forward Christ to atone for the sins that made them sinners in the first place, Romans 3:24-26. For our purposes today we need not concern ourselves with whether the Greek word *hilasterion* in 3:25 should be rendered "expiation" (RSV), "propitiation" (ESV), "sacrifice of atonement" (NIV), or "mercy-seat" (another possible meaning). The point is that since the very sins for which sinners ought to be condemned have been atoned for, expiated, done away, God is entirely right, entirely just, when he declares sinners righteous. But they are found righteous, not in the ordinary sense of the word, because they have acted righteously and done what they ought, but extraordinarily, because even though they have sinned, their sins have been atoned for by the death of Christ. Their declaration of righteousness is thus itself a righteous declaration at the same time as it is a gift of God's grace and not their own achievement.

Fourth: another way of saying that God declares sinners righteous is to say that God forgives their sins. In the opening verses of Romans 4, Paul cites two Old Testament texts in support of the righteousness of faith, apart from the righteous deeds that, in the ordinary understanding of the term, are what make one righteous. The first text concerns Abraham, to whom righteousness was reckoned as a gift because he did not work but trusted the one who declares righteous the ungodly. The second text comes from Psalm 32: "So also David pronounces a blessing upon the one to whom God reckons righteousness apart from works: 'Blessed are those whose iniquities are forgiven, and whose sins are covered; blessed is the one against whom the Lord will not reckon his sins.'" The Old Testament text speaks of God forgiving sins. Paul cites it in support of the claim that God declares people righteous apart from works. How does the text support the claim? Ordinarily, one would expect God to find people righteous because they have done righteous works. But the righteousness of those whose sins are forgiven has a different character ("apart from works"). God finds sinners righteous by forgiving their sins — again, we may add, because "Christ died for our sins."

Fifth: with the effective coming of the righteousness of faith, the ineffectiveness of the righteousness of the law is openly declared, and the law as a path to righteousness comes to an end: "For Christ is the end of the law for righteousness, granted to every one who believes" (Rom. 10:4). The law, with its basic principle — "The one who does these things will live by them" — was never viable as a path to righteousness for *sinners*, but it does define the moral world in which we live. God made human beings moral, and if they are to live and enjoy his blessing in the world as he made it, they must do what is right, they must keep the law. Human beings do not lose their moral obligations simply because they do not fulfill them. And the law rightly reminded them of those obligations.

Now Paul does not fault the Jewish people for pursuing the righteousness of the law. The problem is rather that sinners do not, and cannot, truly submit to God's law. The innocence of Eden, where love of God and walking with God were the spontaneous way of life of unfallen human beings, has now been lost: even the good done by fallen human beings comes short of the innocence of Eden; even the good done by fallen human beings is tainted by sin.

Where Paul *does* fault the majority of his contemporary Jews is for their failure to acknowledge God's righteousness as revealed in Christ, and their continued pursuit of a righteousness based on law after it has been shown to be bankrupt. That is the point of Romans 10:3-4: "Being ignorant of the righteousness that comes from God, and seeking to establish their own, they did not submit to God's righteousness. For Christ is the end of the law for righteousness, granted to every one who believes." The charge is repeated in 2 Corinthians 3: the veil that hides the passing away of the glory of the old order remains in place in the case of unbelieving Jews; only when they turn to Christ is it done away. And the same charge underlies what Paul says in Galatians 3 about the law as valid only until the seed should come to whom the promise had been made, and about how the law served as a custodian until Christ came. It was never wrong to strive to obey God's law. But it is emphatically wrong to believe that one can be righteous that way — now that God has revealed in Christ the path to righteousness through faith.

Sixth: the question has long been asked, does justification mean that God *makes* sinners righteous, or merely that he *declares* them to be righteous? I have used the language of "declaring righteous" throughout my lecture; now I need to explain and defend that language.

A number of interpreters conveniently sidestep the whole question today by saying that the language of righteousness is relational, not moral.[7] To be righteous merely means to be on good terms with God, to be a member of his covenant people, to be part of God's family. When we understand the word this way, it follows that God really does "make" sinners "righteous": he establishes a relationship of being on good terms with them,

---

7. E.g., James D. G. Dunn, *The Theology of Paul the Apostle* (Grand Rapids: Eerdmans Publishing Co., 1998), p. 344.

he takes them into his family, he declares them to be part of his people. But nothing is implied about their moral status. It is a cute explanation, and it does avoid the whole problem, but we should not be buying it. As we have seen, the language of righteousness pertains to our moral obligations. The righteous, in the ordinary sense of the word, are those who meet those responsibilities; the unrighteous are those who do not. And the remarkable point Paul makes by using this language is that God declares people who have not fulfilled their moral obligations nonetheless to be righteous when he forgives their sins. Are they then "made" righteous, or merely "declared" to be so? The question itself is misleading. Those whose sins are wiped away can rightly be considered innocent, or righteous. At the same time, it must be stressed that Paul's focus, when he speaks of justification by faith, is not on the transformation of character that necessarily accompanies justification, but, as we have seen, on the divine acquittal and forgiveness of sins.

Seventh: Paul's message of righteousness by faith raises questions of its own. If righteousness is granted freely to sinners as a gift of God's grace, do sinners declared righteous in this *extraordinary* way have any reason to be righteous in the *ordinary* sense of the word? Why *be* righteous if one is declared righteous anyway by God's grace? Shall we not sin, that grace may abound? (Rom. 6:1).

Let it first be said that the problem arises only when we understand justification along the same lines as Luther. If the modern revisionist reading of Paul were correct, and Paul meant only that Gentiles did not have to be circumcised to eat together with Jewish believers, then no one would have thought he was encouraging people to sin so that grace could abound. But the question is inevitably provoked by the claim that God in his grace declares sinners righteous: if *that* is the case, the cynical wonder, why would anyone bother doing what is right?

The question can be answered, and Paul himself addresses it, in a variety of ways. For our purposes, I want to join Luther in focusing on how a proper understanding of faith makes continuation in sin inconceivable. The Christian life, Paul tells us, begins with faith, in response to God's call heard in the proclamation of the gospel. It is then lived, as it began, in faith. "The life I now live in the flesh I live by faith in the Son of God, who loved me and gave himself for me" (Gal. 2:20). "We walk by faith, not by sight" (2 Cor. 5:7). Faith involves the utter dependence of the believer on God for strength in his or her own ever-present weakness, for hope in his or her own ever-sensed emptiness, for life in the midst of the daily dying that marks all earthly life. We are saved only by grace through faith; and we live only by grace, through faith. Like love and hope, faith abides forever.

But one cannot turn to Christ in faith without at the same time turning away from the sin that alienates us from Christ. In that sense, repentance is inherent in the very nature of faith, an essential element of what faith is all about. And a life of faith in Christ is inevitably expressed in a life of obedience to Christ. We are not living by faith in Christ when we disobey Christ and choose instead to do what we want to do. In that case, we are trusting and following our own judgment rather than his. Only those who obey Christ trust Christ. Where there is no obedience, there is no faith. That is why, in Romans, Paul can speak of the goal of his mission as the "obedience of faith" among all the Gentiles (1:5; 16:26). It is obedience that expresses faith. And true faith in Christ inevitably leads to service for Christ; that is why, in 1 Thessalonians, Paul can speak of the "work of faith" (1 Thess. 1:3). Faith in the One who loved us and gave himself for us inevitably leads to a life of love in response. That is why, in Galatians, Paul can say that, in the end, all that matters is faith expressing itself in love (Gal. 5:6).

But let the last word be Luther's:

Faith, however, is a divine work in us which changes us and makes us to be born anew of God, John 1[:12-13]. It kills the old Adam and makes us altogether different men, in heart and spirit and mind and powers; and it brings with it the Holy Spirit. O it is a living, busy, active, mighty thing, this faith. It is impossible for it not to be doing good works incessantly. It does not ask whether good works are to be done, but before the question is asked, it has already done them, and is constantly doing them. Whoever does not do such works, however, is an unbeliever...

Faith is a living, daring confidence in God's grace, so sure and certain that the believer would stake his life on it a thousand times. This knowledge of and confidence in God's grace makes men glad and bold and happy in dealing with God and with all creatures. And this is the work which the Holy Spirit performs in faith. Because of it, without compulsion, a person is ready and glad to do good to everyone, to serve everyone, to suffer everything, out of love and praise to God who has shown him this grace. Thus is it impossible to separate works from faith.[8]

In short, those who are found righteous by faith are righteous, not in the ordinary sense of the word, because they have done what is right, but in the extraordinary sense that God declares them righteous because Christ has atoned for their sins. But the faith that is extraordinarily counted to them as righteousness then expresses itself in deeds that are righteous in the ordinary sense of the word. Otherwise it is not faith. Modern scholars have rightly reminded us of the nature of the first-century crisis that led Paul to formulate the principle, "No one is justified by works of the law, but by faith in Jesus Christ." Regrettably, they have misinterpreted the formula itself and thus Paul's reason for insisting that Gentile believers must not submit to the law. A law that demands righteous behavior as its path to righteousness is of no use to sinners. But God declares sinners righteous, apart from righteous works, when they respond in faith to the gospel. On that essential point, Luther read Paul aright.

---

8. *Preface to the Epistle of St. Paul to the Romans* (*Luther's Works* 35 [ed. E. Theodore Bachmann; Philadelphia: Muhlenberg Press, 1960]), pp. 370-371.

Law, Gospel and the Beloved Community

Paul R. Hinlicky

Can we gain a fresh take on ecclesiology in the light of the law-gospel debate? I believe that some of the early writings of Dietrich Bonhoeffer can give Lutheran theology today that fresh approach. Twenty years ago arguments over ecclesiology blew the opportunity at the Call to Faithfulness conferences for confessional Lutherans from across denominational lines to unite at a critical juncture in North American history. What follows is dedicated not only to developing a fresh approach to the problem of the church in Lutheran theology, but is given urgency by this all the more precarious moment in history.

Action and Being

We can gain a fresh take on ecclesiology by asking, in Pauline idiom, What is the relation of coming to faith in Christ and being in Christ? We could ask the same question in Johannine fashion by asking how coming to believe that Jesus is the Christ, the Son of God, connects with abiding in Jesus and His word. Or, again, in the Synoptic optic, by inquiring how the Lord's commandments coordinate: 'Repent and believe; the Reign of God draws near,' and, 'This is My Body, given for you; Do this in remembrance of me.' The three major groups of New Testament literature exhibit this same pattern of relating two distinct aspects, action and being, of the gospel and I will treat the New Testament witness as one in this regard in what follows. What we have is a calling out of this dying world and a calling into new life in Christ; a separation and a new assembly; becoming a Christian, which happens one by one in the Spirit's gift of the new birth by Holy Baptism and staying a Christian, which happens as we gather together as church to proclaim the Lord's death until he comes again by the *koinonia* of his Body and Blood. So how do these relate? That is the question before us. Let's unpack the question a bit further by way of introduction.

Coming to faith in Christ is some kind of action, indeed divine action. That is why we insist in Lutheran theology that faith in Christ happens to us by grace, it comes as a gift, it is the action and gift of the Holy Spirit working through the Word, and the Word's visible form, Baptism. This coming to faith, moreover, comes about incalculably, as Augsburg Confession V insists, where and when it pleases God so to work through Word and Sacrament. Being in Christ by contrast designates a state into which one has entered, a continuity, a persistence, a perseverance through time to eternity — this too, of course, by divine action and grace, in that he who has begun a good work in you will not fail to bring it to completion. Abiding in Jesus is abiding in the word of Jesus that the Holy Spirit, the Advocate, continually brings to mind and by which he leads the community to all truth; it is being branches rooted in the vine that is Jesus. When the proclaimer, Jesus, becomes the proclaimed, Jesus Christ, repentance and faith at the nearness of God's reign becomes the gathering together to eat his Body broken for us and to drink his Blood poured out for us. Such being, abiding, feeding in Christ, as per Jesus' own promise, happens predictably, if I may use such a strong word, to indicate the very purpose and goal of God. Consequently, Augsburg Confession VII insists that there is and will be one holy church forever against which the gates of hell shall not prevail.

But what links these two, the free making of each Christian and the assured keeping of Christian community? How do they go together so that we do not play action against being or being against action? Or individual against community or community against individual?

If we polarize these two, we get deformations, either an activist church of restless doers or a static church of stick-in-the-mud stay-putters and in neither case then do we honor the free and faithful grace of God. In the activist church (let the reader understand) *our hands replace God's work* — she who has ears to hear, let her hear! Here the church is nothing but a tool, always getting captured for someone's agenda. In the static church, human traditions quench the Spirit because we circle the wagons to protect our little piece of ever shrinking turf against religious competitors and a hostile world. Here the church becomes a mighty fortress rather than the loving anticipation for the whole world of the beloved community of the Lord who alone is our mighty fortress. So with the antagonistic dualism of action and being we are handed over to all of our traditional, debilitating binaries: evangelical or catholic, low church or high church, pietist or orthodox, liberal or conservative. If we find the way to think these things together, however, maybe we can find again *sanctorum communio*, the communion of people made holy in holy things by the Holy Spirit, where saints are just those worldlings who have been called out and called together by the coming of the Spirit and faith.

Here the free and faithful grace of God would be honored in both the doing and the being, because, if I may cite St. Thomas Aquinas, as cited by the lay Catholic theologian Ralph Del Colle, our belief in 'one holy Church' is "directed to the Holy Spirit, Who sanctifies the Church; so that the sense is: 'I believe in the Holy Spirit sanctifying the Church.'" There you have in a nutshell an answer to the question of what links action and being. The Holy Spirit links being and doing, the One who keeps being and doing together — just as Martin Luther also explained the Third Article: "I believe that I cannot by my own reason or understanding believe in my Lord Jesus Christ or come to Him, but the Holy Spirit has called me by the gospel ... just as He calls, gathers, enlightens, and makes holy the whole Christian church on earth and keeps it with Jesus Christ in the one, common, true faith." As we shall see, the Holy Spirit does just this by the purposeful proclamation of God's law and God's gospel.

As mentioned at the outset, we may recognize in this introductory analysis of the question before us the work of the early Dietrich Bonhoeffer, whose doctoral dissertation had the title,

Sanctorum Communio, and whose next major work, *Act and Being*, diagnosed this problem for a Lutheran theology of the church of overcoming a false and crippling dualism of act and being that in either case removes God the Holy Spirit as the agent in both action and being and thus reduces the church to a human doing or a human being. That is where we are headed in this presentation. But I want to get there with you today in a more accessible way than Bonhoeffer did in the incredibly insightful, yet also incredibly dense writings of his youth. I want to start instead where Luther left off, continue where the *Formula of Concord* left off, and only then come to Bonhoeffer's ecclesiological insight. But having now explored our topic, I can announce a thesis borrowed from Bonhoeffer: *It is the divine presence of Jesus Christ as the Man for Others that at once makes each Christian a disciple and keeps Christians together as his own Body in the world.* Thus far Bonhoeffer, to which I now add: *Christ accomplishes this doing and being by his Spirit's purposeful proclamation of law and gospel.* That is to say: the right proclamation of law and gospel is ordered by the Spirit to being in Christ; calling to faith in Christ purposes being in Christ to the glory of the Father and the world's salvation.

To demonstrate this thesis, I need to show, first, that for Luther, there is an indispensable ordering principle to the relation of Law and Gospel. It is expressed in his Latin by the purpose clause that is introduced with the particle, *ut*, "in order that." God does an *opus alienum, ut faciat opus proprium*. God does an alien work, by the Law indicting, judging and executing *in order to* do his proper work, by the gospel showing mercy, justifying and vivifying. This little particle, *ut*, taken as an ordering principle yields two crucial clarifications about the proper distinction and relation of law and gospel: 1) under discussion here is not human legalism or human antinomianism, but *God*, *God's* action, what *God* is doing in the Law and in the Gospel; 2) thus further, that God's devastating action in the Law to undo the sinner is incomprehensible violence (thus, something *demonic*) if it is not ordered to God's merciful justification and vivification. Going back to Luther himself, the recovery of this ordering principle constitutes the first step I wish to trace on the way to Bonhoeffer's fresh ecclesiological proposal.

I need to show, second, how this purpose clause is lifted up at the conclusion of the *Formula of Concord*, in its final article XI, as the very key to the comforting and strengthening doctrine of God's predestination of us in Christ to be his beloved children and therewith the revelation, according to Ephesians 1, of the mysterious purpose of God in creating, redeeming and fulfilling the world: namely, the coming and the eternal triumph of the Beloved Community. This Beloved Community in Christ is the true object of God's foreordination in all things, not some double list of the damned and the saved. Thus the *action* of God the Holy Spirit in the purposeful proclamation of law and gospel is ordered to our *being* in the eternal life of the Triune God now and forever. What we say about the church finds it proper place within this eternal and divine self-determination, the economy of salvation revealed in the canonical Genesis-to-Revelation narrative.

Law and Gospel in Luther's Last Lecture

Let's begin the demonstration of this thesis where Luther left off. The last public lecture of Martin Luther's academic career, just three months before his death, took place on November 17, 1545. It was the concluding lecture of his decade long series on the Book of Genesis, comprising more or less what is published as the commentary on Chapter 50. Poignantly, Luther concluded with the words: "I can do no more. I am weak. Pray God for me that He may grant me a good and blessed last hour." When we reflect on this, we realize that in the final lecture Luther took occasion to deliver his swan song on law and gospel, to proclaim his last will and theological testament on the crucial and elusive art of properly relating and properly distinguishing law and gospel. What prompted him to do so in the Genesis text is the worry expressed by the brothers, following father Jacob's death: "It may be that Joseph will hate us and pay us back for all the evil which we did to him." This worry induces Luther immediately to remark: "You see here what a horrible evil and what an almost incurable wound sin and an evil conscience are." He then likens the pastoral theologian to a medical doctor whose healing art attends to such wounds of the spirit. I summarize and analyze Luther's last lecture on law and gospel thematically in the following way.

First, *beloved community*. Luther notes that "for 17 years, [these brothers had] received many great blessings from [Joseph], and experienced grace and mercy without intermission, as though he were their father. They had seen and felt his *philadelphia* in the fact that he loved his brothers and cherished them most affectionately." He is speaking of how Joseph forgave his brothers and rejoiced to rescue them from the famine and to restore fellowship when they and all their families migrated to Egypt. Reconciliation restores beloved community. Yet somehow these 17 years of shalom seem not wholly to be real to the brothers. They wonder if it was only for the sake of aged father Jacob that Joseph has put up with them and has not exacted revenge. Luther remarks: "Their hearts are still disturbed, and they are so tormented by their consciousness of their crime and the sting of death that they cannot trust the man who has deserved so well of them." Thus it is under the presupposition that beloved community is both the basis and the goal of reconciliation with God and one another that Luther's analysis of the art of timely and pertinent proclamation of law and gospel takes place.

Second, the *horror of sin*. "Therefore is sin not a horrible thing?" Luther asks. Not just the earthly crime that the brothers committed years before when out of envy they sold their brother Joseph into slavery. That kind of sin, the visible crime that human eyes can see and judge, Luther remarks, "is easily permitted, especially when there are no trials and people sin without fear and with the greatest freedom and smugness." The horror of sin is not only such crime, horrible enough as it is. But that is not the horror Luther has in mind here, which is rather "the great difficulty" with which the "heart longs for the kindness of pardon from God, from whom it [instead] flees and turns away by nature when it feels that He has been offended by many great and enormous sins." This flight from

God compounds sin with more sin and this compounding of sin in unbelief is the "sharp poison," that Luther is pointing at. Not even Joseph's forgiveness and manifest good will for seventeen years overcome it. For sin is a problem with God — a horrible, self-compounding problem.

Third, *the law's impotence and its power*. The law gives no remedy for this poisonous and hellish evil, because it is rather the law's divine work to revive and reveal this "very poison of sin." Given the divine prohibition of envy, of betrayal, and of murder they cannot believe in Joseph's mercy and forgiveness in spite of seventeen years experience of it, in other words, they cannot believe that Joseph's mercy is God's own immutable mercy, divine and certain forgiveness. So the brothers are like "many who do not hear the Word of grace [and] are driven to despair... for they are not able to bear the power of sin when it has been revealed and is alive." Let us learn, writes Luther, "that sin is a horrible evil, not when it is committed — for then it gives pleasure and satisfaction in a strange way — but that when it has been revived through the Law, it is hell itself and far more powerful than heaven and earth...." Sin, not the crime, but the crime's sinfulness is "doubt, unbelief, and hatred for or flight from God...." who by the Law exposes, judges and condemns this flight. God is the One who knows and judges the heart, who seeks and finds all who would flee and hide. That is what Luther means by the "law," the almighty and all-knowing Creator in the office of judge, true and just, before whom no secrets are hid.

Fourth, *the grace of Christ*. Hence, before God the judge the grace of Christ is not and cannot be a mere idea, an "opinion conceived on the basis of human persuasion," as Luther puts it in criticizing notions of faith as merely *notitia*, not self-entrusting *fiducia*. No, here we need a stronger medicine and antidote to meet and defeat the horrible poison of sin than mere ideas, even true ideas such as that God is loving. Here the grace of Christ arrives on the scene, not as an abstract idea, a so-called Christian idea of God as love or grace or any other such abstract sentimentality, for the holy love of God, according to

Luther, is a fiery furnace and severe mercy (Augustine), a divine love that hates what is evil, that hates sin and condemns it. *No*, here the grace of Christ must come as power to defeat power and as justice to defeat injustice in an historical event. As Luther graphically expresses it (forever to the chagrin of refined taste), grace comes as the "blood of the Son of God": "Medicine and help as powerful as this are required, namely, the Godhead become incarnate and the very blood of the Son of God" — divine power and justice respectively. Only this grace of Christ in the flesh is and can be "as new to me now as if He had shed his blood at this hour...," since it is at this very hour that I am in need, found out and judged by God at work through His law, just as I am, all alone with my guilt, without one plea except the new justice of Christ who loved me and gave himself for me.

Fifth, *faith*. Faith, as we have just heard, is not the mere opinion that God is gracious, an opinion which is cheap and cheap covering for persistence in sin, suppression of the knowledge of the truth, and flight from the true God. Faith is not knowledge of the historical fact that 2000 years ago Christ died for us or even belief that Christ's death avails for original sin or past sins. But faith, Luther writes, comes upon the contrite and stricken brothers as they move from introspection to extraspection, so to say, learning to look away from themselves to the bronze serpent lifted up by God. In extraspection it is "not that the memory of sin is completely destroyed," but rather that the "conscience is not tortured but knows that it has the forgiveness of sins and eternal life through Christ." How is this extraspection of faith possible? Christ in his grace must come to them! How does he come to them? Luther's Joseph, in his holy sufferings and eventual vindication by which God worked the salvation of many, is a type of Christ, and now, as a type of Christ, Joseph preaches his own forgiveness of his brothers to them as God's very forgiveness: "If God has pardoned you, if you have a good conscience and are sure of His pardon and forgiveness, why should you have doubts about me? For I am not above God, am I? Remain with me under God...." Return to our beloved community, your sins are born away by the Lamb of God, truly away. The poison has been drawn, the horror met and vanquished for you. So is born Luther's faith, justifying faith, as he so often expressed it in his picture of the joyful exchange, where the risen and present Christ declares, "I am yours and you are mine. I take your sins and give you my righteousness." Faith concurs to just this personal promise made in the flesh by the One who comes to rob us of our sins and replace them with the new and powerful justice of his own self-giving sacrifice. Accordingly we may say with Dietrich Bonhoeffer about justifying faith: only such faith obeys because only such obedience believes in the present Christ who is really there for us — even before God.

Sixth, *the theodicy of faith*. But we can press the question even further with Luther. Why should the brothers give up their horror and be reconciled to God as also to Joseph, even taken as the type of Christ? How can they believe Joseph's forgiveness, or Christ's forgiveness, as God's when it contradicts God's just judgment on their crime, not to mention their sinful flight from just this divine reckoning? Luther gives the reason why they can believe when he writes how Joseph now "adds an exceedingly serious statement: 'It is indeed true that you meant evil against me, but God is wonderful in His counsels and has turned your worst thoughts to our advantage and the greatest good....'" Many would have died of hunger in the famine, in other words, had not God used your evil plan for his own good and saving purpose. Luther connects Joseph's interpretation in faith of God's purpose supervening his sufferings with Romans 8: "We know that all things work together for good to them that love God, to them that are called according to his purpose." Recalling that Joseph is for Luther a type of Christ, then, the good reason why the brothers can believe that the forgiveness of Joseph, the very victim of their own crime, is indeed God's forgiveness is that Joseph himself, standing for Christ, has received his innocent suffering from God in love and obedience for the sake of many, even for his guilty brothers. What an awesome and unheard of righteousness! Joseph justifies God in his obedient faith. By this spiritual obedience many are justified; this precisely is Paul's argument about the validity of Christ's obedience for us all in Romans 5, which atones for us all. At Gethsemane, Christ received his own suffering from God for the sake of others. They meant it for evil, but God meant it for good. This I call the theodicy of faith.

Luther further connects the "wonderful counsel" of God with Augustine's theodicy from the *City of God*, "God is so good that He does not permit evil to be done unless He can draw great good from it." This is wisdom, to be sure, of the Spirit and only for faith. It is not philosophy or philosophical theodicy; it is the theodicy *of faith*. Otherwise, we shall scornfully infer that God is the author of evil and ask, "Shall we sin then that grace may abound?" "Why not do evil that good may come?" Immediately and with no little passion, Luther fends off this unspiritual inference of the unbelieving philosopher who hears the thought, but not as one who loves God or is called according to God's purpose. Oh no, Luther replies, "God certainly detests and hates sin," and his purpose is for you "to flee for refuge to Christ the Savior, who does not want the death of a sinner, just as He does not want a sinner either." God causes good to result from evil, resurrection from crucifixion, not that he wants evil to be done, but rather "His goodness is so great that even in our wickedness He cannot do otherwise than forgive sin if the sinner sobs and implores His mercy." By the same token the "danger" remains that "those who are without fear will be seized by death and descend into hell before they can flee for refuge to God's mercy." The theodicy of faith thus includes true contrition or repentance; it is the very judgment in faith by them that love God according to God's own purpose. In this ultimate perspective, however, we do see how justifying faith is a Gethsemane of the soul that in Christ obediently justifies God in his judgment, trusting in his mercy. Just so, "when consolation has been grasped, sin already has been cured." A new being has been born.

Finally, according to Luther, this new being in Christ walks the royal road between pride and despair. Spiritual pride is legalism, the presumption that one can and does fulfill the law without the mediation of Christ and the gift of the Spirit. Spiritual despair is antinomianism, the abandonment of oneself to sin as either helpless to do otherwise or as fated to failure and condemnation. One or the other overtakes us when we do not let the law be God's holy law, by which the Holy Spirit reveals the poison as poison so that he may heal. Once again invoking Augustine, Luther resolves the theodicy of faith into the practical maxim: "one should fear God. He hates both presumption and despair." Luther's final counsel to the believer runs: "Therefore you should not sin rashly, confident of obtaining God's pardon; but you should rely on this pardon and find rest in it only when you are in despair." His corresponding admonition to pastors is that they should "give assistance; and mercy, which is far greater than sin, should be glorified."

Let me summarize this way: Luther orders law and gospel with the purpose clause of the Holy Spirit, as we hear again and again throughout the Genesis commentary. For example, through the Holy Scriptures, Luther writes, the "Holy Spirit speaks to us in this manner: 'I am a God who kills and brings to life, brings down to Sheol and raises up, makes poor and makes rich (cf. 1 Sam. 2:6-7). Not separately or disjunctively. Killing is not the only thing I do. No, this would be devilish. But I am a God who kills and brings back to life. I bring down to Sheol, but in such a way that I bring back....' [This] is the special wisdom and teaching of the Christians...." Or again, "God wants you to be humbled, not to perish. He is not angry with you. Nor has He hurled this thunderbolt against you in His rage. No, it has been His purpose to lead you to knowledge of your sins and to buoy you up and strengthen you when you have been humbled." Note now two consequences. If, first, we presented a *Deus absconditus*, One who finally only kills, or kills and makes alive indifferently or capriciously or purposelessly, that would not simply be bad theology, or even heresy; it would be *devilish* — the work of the unholy spirit! Thus, second, when Luther says that God is "exempt" from the Law and that he should not be "subjected to it" because "He is its Lord and can manage and act otherwise than the Law commands," the sense is not *a priori* put *a posteriori*, not ethical but juridical. God is not bound to execute the sinner, end of story, since in fact God finds the way both powerful and just in the cross and resurrection of Jesus Christ to turn human evil to his good, merited condemnation to unmerited justification, death to life. The God whom Luther discovers in his christological reading of the Joseph story is not in principle a *deus exlex*, an arbitrary God, but a *Deus supra legem*, God beyond law. And God surpasses his own holy law in Christ's death and resurrection, figured in Joseph's innocent suffering for the sake of God's beloved community, when trusting Joseph owned that suffering sent upon him from God for the sake of others, even those worthy only of punishment for their crimes. By this christological mediation and joyful exchange, God shows himself Lord also of the law which must now serve the purpose of the Holy Spirit for beloved community.

The *Formula of Concord*'s Last Article

I introduce this next section on FC XI into our considerations in order both to confirm the preceding understanding from Luther of God's law as ordered to God's gospel and to move our understanding of the ordering principle, the purpose clause, at once *back* to God's eternal self-determination to create, redeem and fulfill the world through the missions of the Son and the Spirit and *forward* then to the act and being of the church as harbinger of eternal life in God's beloved community. FC XI, the concluding article of the Formula, expressly states that it does not propose to settle any intra-Lutheran disputes as the preceding ten articles do. Rather it expresses an early Lutheran consensus. Looking out at the looming schism among the Reformed over predestination that will eventually erupt between the orthodox Calvinist doctrine of double predestination on the one side and the Arminian doctrine of free will on the other, FC XI attempts preventative medicine, "to prevent disunity and schism over these issues" of "the eternal election of the children of God." But that is not the only motive. The formulators are just as convinced that "no one should ignore or reject this teaching of the divine Word just because some have misused and misunderstood it" and so they propose to "explain the proper understanding of it on the basis of Scripture." The reason for this conviction, I submit, is that the eternal election of the children of God provides us the theological grounding of that ordering principle of law and gospel. The beloved community in Christ is God's goal in creating, redeeming and fulfilling the world; the proper distinction and relation of law and gospel is thus a distinction within this divine economy.

Indeed, FC XI concludes just where we left off with Luther, forbidding pride and despair alike. "By instructing people to seek eternal election in Christ and in his holy gospel as the Book of Life, this teaching gives no one cause either for faintheartedness or for a brazen, dissolute life. For this teaching excludes no repentant sinners. Instead, it calls and draws all poor, burdened, and trouble sinners to repentance, to the recognition of their sins, and to faith in Christ. It promises the Holy Spirit for purification and renewal. Thus, it gives the most reliable comfort to troubled, tempted people, that they may know that their salvation does not rest in their own hands... [but] in the gracious election of God." Just like we heard from Luther, then, it is "devilish" whenever this purpose clause is not working to order the proclamation of law to gospel. The formulators, citing the Apostle's statement that all Scripture is written that we might have hope, stipulate that any presentation of the doctrine of election that produces pride or despair "is not being presented according to God's Word and will but rather according to reason and at the instigation of the devil."

At the same time, the formulators advance the case for this ordering principle beyond its rudiments worked out by Luther. They do so by several crucial moves. They begin with a daring argument that violates the venerable principle of divine simplicity that had driven Zwingli and the orthodox followers of Calvin by logical necessity, the doctrine of the eternal divine reprobation of the wicked. Divine simplicity means that God is simply one in knowing, willing, and doing. So if anyone is damned, God has known it, willed it and done it. Against this principle of divine simplicity, the formulators demand that we "carefully note the difference between God's eternal foreknowledge and his eternal election of his children," the first understood as an act of divine intelligence which knows all things in advance but the second as an act of divine love by which God determines himself towards creatures in one way and not another. The formulators say there is a difference here, that God is not simply one in knowing and willing. Thus according to these early Lutherans God can know and permit that Adam will sin but not properly will it, just as God can foresee and determine that Jesus will be crucified but not desire or author the malice and injustice of his crucifiers. According to the doctrine of simplicity, however, this Lutheran distinction is quite impossible. There can be no real difference between God's knowing and God's willing; in God both are simply one and the same. God knows what he wills and wills what he knows, otherwise he would not be God.

If divine simplicity is true in this way, there are indeed only limited options. One would be to limit God's governance, like Plato did, and say that God can't help it. God is only good, not powerful; God is limited by the material he has to work with, which is at fault in failure or sin. Or, as Christian Platonism argued, for example, in Luther's beloved Augustine, one could say that God is alone really real, hence evil is unreal to him and thus cannot affect God. At the same time, if one sees that evil is actual on the earth, and if one is unwilling to give up God's governance over all things, there seems to be no other conclusion to be drawn by Christian Platonism from the evident fact that many are called but few are chosen than that God properly wills also the loss of those not chosen, as Augustine sometimes darkly suggests and as Zwingli picked up and argued in principle in his treatise against Luther *On the Providence of God*. The Lutheran formulators, however, mock this conception of God's election and reprobation as an absolute divine decree. They compare it to a military "muster, in which God said, 'this one shall be saved, that one shall be damned; this one will remain faithful, that one will not remain faithful.'" They assert instead that God's preordination "does not apply to both the godly and the evil, but instead only to the children of God, who are chosen and predestined to eternal life 'before the foundation of the world'" as elaborated in Ephesians 1. Thus, while God surely foresees sin and its evil consequences, God hates and rejects the sin he foresees and does not desire it, will it, purpose it or author it. Yet it happens. God permits it.

Note then what this Lutheran view of the divine permission of evil entails: strictly speaking, God suffers. Not of course in the pathetic way of human creatures, but in the spiritual way that befits God as Creator. In creating a world that is genuinely other than God, God suffers the contradiction of wills other than his own that are actual and do actual violence to God's name as well as the creation's goodness. That is why Paul the Apostle speaks of the long-suffering patience of God. God is not surprised by sin, but sin occurs as a real effect in the world, e.g., the crime of the brothers in selling Joseph into slavery and their ensuing flight from God's judgment as discussed in the previous section. It does real damage, not only to creatures, but to God's name and authority in the world. In such a world, the victory of the Triune God is the accomplishment of his determination from the beginning in Christ by the Spirit to turn our evil to his good. This, according to the formulators, is what God predestines, the final victory of the beloved community, including even us ungodly as nevertheless beloved children. Just as we saw Luther interpreting the Joseph story, the Lutheran view of election is that God is not surprised by the sin that He does not will. But reckoning with it from all eternity as the very cost of creating us, God's own self-determination is to redeem and fulfill the very earth on which the cross of his Son would stand. God permits evil that he does not will in order to accomplish his own good purpose from out of its ruins. Whoever comes to this judgment in faith — that God receives me the sinner for the sake of Christ — experiences divine election.

Building on Luther, the approach of the formulators thus articulates four new things. First, "God's counsel, intention, and preordination in Jesus Christ (who is the genuine, true 'Book of Life') is revealed to us through the Word. This means that the entire teaching of God's intention, counsel, will, and preordination concerning our redemption, calling, justification and sanctification must be taken as a unity." Jesus Christ is not God's second thought, his "Oh gee, Adam sinned, what do I do now?" Creation is not a neutral, empty stage on which a human drama unfolds one way or another. But creation is part and parcel of one will of God in Jesus Christ to redeem and fulfill a world other than God for communion with God. Second, in Jesus Christ, accordingly, there is and can be no deception, no pretense as if outwardly God calls by the gospel but inwardly were play acting with someone already secretly fated to death. God is true in his self-giving in Christ and self-revealing by the Spirit. Third, the "human race has been truly redeemed and reconciled with God...," the "promise of the gospel is *universalis*, that is, it pertains to all people." The notion of a limited atonement only for the elect gets thing precisely backwards: all are included in Christ's atoning death; election in this One rejected for us is universal; only self-exclusion that persists in owning sin rather than surrendering it to the Lamb of God remains as a mysterious final possibility. Fourth, God's permission of evil in the kenosis of creation, so to say, is just this mysterious final possibility of God's suffering sinners to have their way eternally, letting them exercise their powers just as they see fit, forever. That would be hell.

This is the most difficult point. The formulators allow this kind of human freedom, if such it be called, our freedom in sin to sin forever. "Thus the Apostle very carefully distinguishes between the work of God, who alone makes vessels for honor, and the work of the devil and of human beings, who, at the instigation of the devil and not of God, have made themselves vessels of dishonor." Indeed, "as God is not the cause of sins, so he is also not the cause of punishment or condemnation." Following the Apostle's teaching in Romans 1:18ff, they teach that God abandons the wicked to their wickedness, "God punishes sin with sin." God permits the evil that he does not will. Yet the reverse does not hold; they deny that there is "something in us" which is "a cause of God's election." So we have a paradox. We are unfree in our election, as Jesus says, "You did not choose Me. I chose you." But we are free in our rejection. In wanting to be the free cause of our existence, we cause our own condemnation as we persist in refusing God's election of the rejected to life in Jesus Christ. Of course, even more paradoxically our unfreedom in election gives us the glorious liberty of the children of God while the so-called freedom to reject the grace of Christ gives persistence, even eternal persistence, in bondage to sin and death. Difficult as that final paradox is, it gives the reason why Jesus in Johannine idiom brings the *krisis* of the world, its on-going, provisional but actual *division*. Just this *krisis* of Jesus who elects in the gospel only those rejected by the law makes and marks the division between the church as harbinger of the Beloved Community and the dying world that flees from God. The church that is not in this sense *against the world* is not holy and has nothing whatsoever to do with Jesus Christ.

When we follow out the theologic of Article XI fully, we come to the eternal counsel and proper will of the Triune God: "for the Holy Spirit wills to be present with his power in the Word and to work through it. This is the drawing of the Father." We see that this "eternal election of God should be considered in Christ and not apart from or outside of Christ. For in Christ, the holy apostle Paul testifies, we have been chosen before the foundation of the world, as it is written, "He has loved us in his Beloved.... Thus the entire Holy Trinity, God the Father, Son and Holy Spirit, directs all people to Christ as the Book of Life, in whom they should seek the Father's eternal election." This beloved community of God, then, is the intention, the purpose, the goal of the Trinity for the creation, the Trinity's own proper self-expression in and for creation. Notice what has happened: in the course of thinking out God's purpose in Christ, the framework of religious individualism with which the late medieval quest for a gracious God began has been transcended, without however abandoning the existential and personal dimension of faith. Rather the redeemed individual has been correlated essentially with the Beloved Community, God's action has been correlated with God's final purpose, shedding light on the church's battle in the fog and friction of human history.

Bonhoeffer's *Sanctorum Communio*

Bonhoeffer's discussion in *Sanctorum Communio* is so rich, so laden with insight, so fruitful for our situation, so suggestive for all of us seeking new directions for Lutheranism and a fresh approach to "life together" that in my remaining space I can hardly do it justice. I am satisfied if, by narrowly discussing it in connection with the themes thus far introduced, I can call this text to attention and urge its study and further exploration.

Just like the Lutheran formulators before him, Bonhoeffer drew on Ephesians 1 to maintain that "the church is God's new will and purpose for humanity... [that] begins to be implemented *in history*." "We experience our election only in the church-community, which is already established by Christ, by personally appropriating it through the Holy Spirit, by standing in the actualized church." Bonhoeffer found in this Lutheran approach to ecclesiology a threefold advantage. First, as just mentioned, it transcends religious individualism and indeed exposes individualism as sin, yet without diminishing the existential seriousness of personal faith. Second, it exposes the being of the church as "Christ existing as community" over against modern political sovereignty, Hobbes' mortal God, the Leviathan, the "being in Adam" that Bonhoeffer sees taking fresh and ominous form in Hitlerism. And third, it renders the ordering principle of the proper distinction of law and gospel that I have been discussing throughout. In Bonhoeffer's own words: "The cord between God and human beings that was cut by the first Adam is tied anew by God, by revealing God's own love in Christ, by no longer approaching us in demand and summons, purely as You [i.e., as in, "Adam where art thou?"], but instead by *giving God's own self as an I, opening God's own heart. The church is founded on the revelation of God's own heart.*" Let's probe these points, beginning with his criticism of individualism.

To be more precise, I should say egoism, both individual and collective. People ask, Bonhoeffer says, "whether the religious community... is a necessary consequence of the Christian religion, or whether Christianity is essentially individualistic." But as posed this question is false because it does not begin with "the reality of God's revelation in Jesus Christ" as that which "simultaneously establishes the church as a reality of revelation." Action of God and Being in God correlate. Indeed, Bonhoeffer continues, "*only the concept of revelation can lead to the Christian concept of the church*," that is to say, "only when faith accepts the meaning of redemption does it become clear what makes this reality [of the church] necessary." Only when God's action in making a Christian is clearly understood is the necessity of being in Christ grasped. The usual question whether religion is collective or individualist trades one kind of egoism for another; but the reality established in Christ by God's act of love is one in which "community is an integral element of its nature." Community here means sharing not just outward association. Bonhoeffer's Christ-existing-as-community, in other words, is not any old collectivity but exactly sharing, God in Christ sharing his divine life with creatures so that creatures share their lives with one another in new "life together." Sharing unifies acting and being. Sharing is the act which gives new life. The sharing, the *koinonia*, the communion of the Holy Spirit makes a Christian when Christ becomes present to take sin and give righteousness and keeps a Christian when the same Spirit bonds each one so claimed by Christ to all the others in beloved community.

These affirmations about the church — neither as institution nor as association but as sharing, as holy community, as joyful exchange — utterly depend on Bonhoeffer's Christology of the real presence and active work of Christ in history: "To be noted is the use of [the Greek] *en* [in] throughout — 'we are reconciled not only by him, but *in him*.' Hence to understand his person and history properly is to understand our reconciliation properly. If we, the members of the Christian church-community, are to believe that in Christ we are reconciled with

God, then the mediator of this reconciliation must represent not only the reconciling divine love, but also at the same time, the humanity that is to be reconciled, the humanity of the New Adam." In lifting up the New Adam aspect of Christology, Bonhoeffer, following Luther following Augustine following Paul, draws here upon the notion of collective person: "In Christ humanity is really drawn into community with God, just as in Adam humanity fell." Although we are all Adam and so there are many Adams, many egoisms, there is only one New Adam, one Christ, one righteous man, Jesus, this Man for Others. His unique and particular action makes sharing the Christian state of being.

In this way Bonhoeffer is able to anticipate and meet the nervous objection to his fresh take on ecclesiology, namely, that Christ existing as community implies that the community swallows up Christ and controls him; that Christology becomes a function of ecclesiology. Remarkably he defeats this objection by retrieving the offense of Luther's sharp teaching on the penal suffering of Jesus Christ as the indigestible stone that forbids and forestalls any such ecclesiastical swallowing.

What "sheds the clearest light on the fundamental difference between Adam and Christ" is Jesus' "*function of vicarious representative.*" "God does not 'overlook' sin; that would mean not taking human beings seriously as personal beings in their very culpability; and that would mean no re-creation of the person, and therefore no re-creation of the community." The penal suffering of Christ is therefore the ultimate, inconceivable act of divine sharing: "in the death of Jesus on the cross God's judgment and wrath are carried out on all the self-centeredness of humanity.... Because he was made sin for us, and because he was accursed by the law for us, Jesus died in solitude." This work of Jesus alone is Jesus' alone. So, "though innocent, Jesus takes the sin of others upon himself." Consequently in obedient faith to Christ's gracious command, 'I take your sin, I give you my righteousness,' we *ought* to share in turn, "we *ought* to let our sin be taken from us, for we are not able to carry it by ourselves; we *ought* not reject this gift of God." Just this passive obedience of our faith brought about by Christ's proffered robbery of our sins, just this trusting and obedient surrender to this divine Robber is *"the reality of the divine love for the church community"* by which it is called out from the world and united in the gift of Christ's own, to us alien, righteousness. The church of forgiven sinners lives in this obedient separation from the world that is dying only because it holds onto its sins and does not share them with Christ. The church of forgiven sinners lives together in sharing, in turn, not by bearing one another's sins, the work of Christ alone, but by sharing one another's burdens.

Notice, then, how Bonhoeffer has related faith in Christ to being in Christ: "Faith is based on entry into the church-community, just as entry into the church-community is based on faith." There is a Trinitarian dialectic at work here: the Word points to the Spirit and the Spirit points to the Word. "Thus Christ and the Holy Spirit are at work in this word; and both are inseparably linked — the Holy Spirit has no other content than the fact of Christ." What the Holy Spirit does in proclaiming the gospel is to make the crucified Christ present to us as the Risen One who robs us of our sins in Word and Sacrament so that we surrender to this divine Thief in the faith which reckons this thievery as God's own new and stunning justice, which gives precisely what we do not deserve. The church-community, in turn, is just this economy on the earth, just this field of joyful exchange. "He who knew no sin was made to be sin in order that in Him we might become the justice of God:" such *becoming* by faith is *being* in Christ.

Law, Gospel and Beloved Community

I draw to a conclusion with the words of Eberhard Jüngel, who notes that our Latin-based word, sacrament, translates Paul's Greek, *mysterion*, the "mystery of God's gracious primal decision for sinners" that in Christ and by the Spirit they would become now and forever the beloved children of God. In Jüngel's felicitious formulation of this line of thought, Jesus Christ is the sacrament of God, and his community is the worldly sign, the element, the material of it in which he abides. In coming to this conclusion, I have shown how Bonhoeffer's ecclesiology is rooted in Luther's ordering principle and in the FC XI's doctrine of our election in Christ as the children of God and how the Lordship of Christ over and in the church is maintained by the uniqueness of Christ's penal suffering for others at the cross.

In the process, we have seen how Bonhoeffer's ecclesiology also worked to purge modern Lutheran law-gospel theology of a vicious though subtle anti-Judaism, influentially extended, for example, in the docetic and antinomian theology of Rudolph Bultmann. Here a shell game took place. The problem of the law of God was reduced to anthropology, to human "boasting" or spiritual "pride," emblematized by Judaism, as if Paul were Marcion and our problem was merely legalism rather than sinful flight from God at work as Judge in his own holy law. But the law of Israel is for Bonhoeffer the holy law of God, by which the Creator calls and judges the called for their fidelity to his calling, that is, as the *ecclesia*, as the church. "The law of God for Israel is the calling properly heard. Law and calling belong together.... Both ideas of God's call and God's law, therefore, point to community." Bonhoeffer is thinking of the preface to the Decalogue, "I am the Lord your God who brought you out of the land of Egypt, out of the house of bondage," the saving act of divine grace which grounds the community in the commandment, "have no other gods before Me." He is as well thinking of Luther's own theological thinking with our Christian Old Testament, as we heard earlier in the commentary on the Joseph story, namely, that the promise, "I am the Lord your God" and the faith which believes it is in principle and in power the obedience that does not merely observe but spiritually fulfills the law, as in holy Joseph, the very type of Christ, though paradoxically in vicarious or representative suffering. "The law," Bonhoeffer explains, "does not establish community [*Gemeinschaft*] but solitude [think of Joseph in prison or Jesus on the cross!] — as a consequence of human sin, of course — for the law is holy and good and was meant to be the norm and pattern of life of a *holy* people of God. The law can only be fulfilled in spirit through spirit, that is, an unbroken will to obey God, i.e., through perfect love."

So, just as Joseph loved the brothers who had betrayed him and restored them to beloved community, so Christ who loves the unlovely overcomes the condemnation of the law by fulfilling its demand for love, even for those unable and unworthy — an action of grace and Spirit that meets and defeats actual sin, real betrayal in real history and thus defeats the law's condemnation not only with power but also with justice. This event and this being are what we should be thinking about with the term "church." Here "the preaching of God's love speaks of the community into which God *has* entered with each and every person — with all those who in utter solitude have known themselves separated from God and other human beings and [yet] believe this message." The Spirit's active assembly of such people by the purposeful proclamation of law and gospel so that we abide in Jesus is here and now on this earth the Father's ever new beginning of the Beloved Community.

Freedom and Obedience in the Christian Life

Piotr J. Malysz

The argument I wish to make in this essay is that freedom and obedience in the Christian life are both determined by the gospel. They are, in fact, two inalienable sides of one and the same evangelical reality. I shall express their indissoluble unity by arguing, more specifically, that the gospel gives a *godly* form to Christian life.

As I argue this point, I shall appeal largely to the thought of Luther. But the important implication of my argument, in the broader context of the Lutheran tradition, is that freedom is not the sole dimension of the gospel, whereas obedience is said to remain in the province of the law, to be spelled out and elicited through its so-called third use. To forestall any hasty charge of antinomianism (a charge that would, in any case, be a misunderstanding of what antinomianism, historically speaking, is), let me emphasize that my skepticism regarding the law's role in structuring Christian obedience in no way means that the law has no role to play for the Christian. It does. Our task will be to specify this role. It is only as a description of, and exhortation to, a Christian life that the law falls decidedly short.

My argument will unfold as follows. I shall, first, examine our present context — that of early twenty-first century Western society — which is often bemoaned as antinomian and with no sense of limits. I shall argue, over against sanative suggestions of imposing a *nomos* on this perceived chaos, that lawlessness is a misdiagnosis and that, consequently, the law is not that which will restore a sense of order, let alone elicit true obedience. Rather, what is needed is the gospel. This claim will, in turn, lead me to examine the impact of the gospel on the person's being, both in the sense of Spirit-worked liberation from the law and in the sense of giving rise to a Christ-like agent. Importantly, the gospel's impact on the person will be shown to have ineluctable social implications. In light of this discussion, I shall then consider the role of commands as expressive of the Christian life. Finally, the concluding section will take up the Christian's active relation to the law. All in all, as the unfolding argument will make clear, the godly form that the gospel gives to the Christian life is, in fact, a life structured by the self-communication of the triune God, a very different kind of life from law-centered spiritualties of human devising.

The Law of Lawlessness

Let me begin with some social observations. It has become *de rigueur* in some circles to bemoan our age as an age of social permissivism, an age of unprecedented moral laxity and, among those theologically informed, an age of antinomianism. The editor of *First Things*, for example, complains in a recent article that "an antinomian spirit predominates in our culture at large." The remedy this and other jeremiads of this sort ordinarily suggest is simple: law, more law. The goal, as R. R. Reno puts it, is "a law-saturated life."

I do wonder, however, whether antinomianism is a precise enough diagnosis of the predicament we are in, and for this reason I also wonder about the suggested remedy. When it comes to the culture at large, the predominant "gospel" out there is that one can (with some exceptions) be oneself. But it seems to me that, contrary to appearances, this news is no good news at all. First, the "can" hides within itself an "ought" — because one can, one must! Second, because the authorization to be oneself is cultural, one can be oneself only within socially determined parameters of what counts as being oneself. We live in a society whose creed, to be sure, is unconditional acceptance, a celebration of diversity, difference, and freedom from artificially imposed constrains that stifle our individuality. Yet ours is also a society that directs even its non-conformists to special stores where they can buy mass-produced clothing just for them. One acts out one's identity — but only according to a socially approved script. One gives expression to one's identity, following a socially respected path of achievement. This disjunction between what *allegedly* is the case and what *really* is the case is responsible for the fact that the basic mode of our social functioning is *self-creation* — self-creation that, in reality, is not a release but a constant corseting of the self, which will not quite fit into its made-to-measure garb.

Because self-creation has this public dimension, it is always self-creation in the face of judgment. One craves others' recognition, and one simultaneously fears that one will be judged to be maladjusted or, even worse, fake, self-hating, and in self-denial. None of us wants to join the ranks of the invisible and the disposable. So we must justify ourselves before others. Like Facebook users (and as Facebook users), we want to feel that we are unique and different, that we are ourselves, but we need this uniqueness explicitly affirmed, given a thumbs-up, shown that what we are, where we are, what we read, what we eat, what we hold dear, etc. — that all that is likeable and worth other people's while.

This process of self-justification for the sake of being justified is perhaps the most acute in its economic dimension. John Milbank, among others, has drawn attention to the manner in which advanced capitalism relies on maintaining people's "formal freedom as subjects," while pushing them down the path of self-commodification and voluntary enslavement. What drives this commodification of the self, I believe, is precisely the promise of having one's self publically affirmed in the safe haven of already recognized products and services. In other words, we rely on commodities and goods sanctioned by the advertising industry, since they are proven to bring out who I really am and simultaneously also guarantee admiration. But the cost to the self — in case we should believe we are still in control — is hardly a one-time compromise. For, just as rapidly, we are instructed to discard those very things as potentially disfiguring. Today's cell-phone testifies to my technological savvy.

Yesterday's cell-phone makes me look uncool, when I know for a fact, and want others to know, that I am a really cool person.

And so, without complaint or question, we submit to the strict regime that promises a radical unveiling of the self. We follow the prescribed paths on a never-ending pilgrimage of self-revelation. We do so, even when the failures we cannot live down and successes we can no longer live up to call into question the whole idea of bringing out the real me — the me that shows itself to be manipulative, delusional, and not all that pretty in high definition. Only now, in a stark reversal, we settle on a safe, socially palatable projection and carry on as before, investing just as much effort into making sure that the real me should never come to light.

But, one might object, the real me often does come to light in all its disfigurement, and does so deliberately. "Today," writes a *First Things* editor, "most of us participate, however half-heartedly, in a permissive cultural sensibility, a pervasive mentality of therapeutic self-affirmation." However, it is not insignificant that people actually feel compelled to submit even their morally questionable acts to the verdict of society. They do so explicitly, by exposing their hearts and bodies for others to see and approve, or implicitly, by invoking social sanction in the form of "Everybody's doing it, anyway." Therapeutic self-affirmation must reckon with the conditions of social affirmation, and cultural permissiveness is governed by rigorous procedures. That our society might be noticeably laxer on questions of "traditional" morality does not alleviate the relentlessness of constantly having to justify oneself in a public forum.

This inescapability of self-justification is further reinforced and complicated by *systemic* uncertainties of the late modern society. As sociologist Zygmunt Bauman points out, today we have no choice but to try as best we can to resolve these uncertainties in our *individual* biographies. We are doomed to make sense of what it means to be oneself in the context of pervasive risks posed by the global economy, transnational power, and the ever-looming uncertainty of the future. This is a tall order, and the obvious impossibility of this task involves us in a contradiction. The contradiction is defined, according to Bauman, by a disjunction between *self-assertion*, from which we cannot withdraw, and *self-constitution* or self-securing, of which we are now decidedly incapable. We have no choice but to keep on going, with no promise of ever getting anywhere and no hope of deliverance.

The important conclusion that we can draw from this all too short a sketch is that, while our society unconditionally recognizes difference, etc., it does not automatically recognize me. This recognition I must achieve, so that it becomes true also *for me*. In this important respect — in the sense that my social visibility and, so to speak, salvation are by no means a given — the antinomianism of the culture at large is at best an antinomianism *de iure* but not *de facto*. For this reason, I remain skeptical of the proposed solution: that more law can provide a way out of the situation, that, as R. R. Reno holds, what one needs is "commandment ... which transforms by providing the means for human life to be brought into accord with God's will." "[D]ivine commandements," Reno argues, "have the ... capacity to effect communion," they are "engines of our intimacy with God." But the idea that a social imposition of another type of order and another type of regime can save us from alleged lawlessness — even if what one ostensibly has in mind is God's own law — strikes me as both naïve and theologically suspicious.

Its naiveté was driven home to me again quite recently, while I was reading an interview with Leon Kasman, a communist official involved in the installation of the system in postwar Poland. Kasman speaks of the government's singular astonishment — yes, astonishment! — at the persistence of prostitution. The communists believed all evil was simply a product of unjust and demoralizing social conditions. They believed that prostitution was merely a hangover from the old system and that it would simply disappear. But it stubbornly did not. "Why?" asks Kasman. "There was no poverty that would force a woman into selling her body. There was always work available. Nor was it the case any more that an unmarried woman who gave birth to a child had either to kill it, or have someone else look after the child, while she took to the street in order to support it. We had orphanages; we had shelters for mothers with children. Where was the problem? ... Or take thieves? Or murderers?"

Saturating life with law, however fitting, dignified, and otherwise perfect one may think this law to be, hardly seems to rectify things in society. It does not afford, as it were, social salvation. When an order is installed as a response to perceived lawlessness, this only endows the order with an aura of finality, as if everything were to be all right from now on, because a law is at last in place. But, in reality, what happens is that one law is pitted against another. One order, rooted in a specific set of values, is pitted against another order, usually rooted in the same, or similar set of values. Love against love; human flourishing against human flourishing. "Value thinking," as Eberhard Jüngel warns, "is thoroughly aggressive.... No one can valuate without devaluing, revaluing, and evaluating." However good a law might be, it cannot do away with the relentlessness of self-justification. It does not put an end to human hypocrisy. And it does not stamp out transgression. Just the opposite: it fuels the relentlessness of self-creation, self-hiding in the face of failure, and resentment against the inescapability of public judgment. More than that, it is from the law that the temptation comes to supplant one type of law with another, more palatable kind, or the kind that we may even believe to be the gospel of salvation as long as everyone is made to obey it. Thus, in short, to protect against apparent antinomianism by determining values and multiplying commandments is not to recognize the *debilitating and oppressive undertow of law that characterizes human existence*. It is to add fuel to the fire.

This move is not only naïve, but it also betrays a theological failure: if we seriously believe that the gospel alone makes humans free, then antinomianism is impossible also from a theological perspective. The culture at large, however antinomian it may seem on the face of it, is really in bondage to law. Luther, too, assumes this broader view of the law. "[T]ake 'works of the Law' generally," he instructs his students, "to mean whatever is opposed to grace: Whatever is not grace is Law, whether it be the Civil Law, the Ceremonial Law, or the Decalog." Or, we might add, the law of social convention and acceptability. True, we may also be a culture of analgesics, as Leszek Kolakowski put it back in the 1960s — a society on painkillers and anti-depressants, obsessively tranquilizing its own conscience. The laws of our apparent lawlessness may also be only laws of our own making. But none of this changes the fact that it is to the law that we are mercilessly delivered up, that it is in the face of law that we constantly try to justify ourselves and make sense of our existence. What we yearn for is the gospel; but what we are able to find is only law, more law, more subtle law, so subtle that we are shackled by its apparent tenuousness.

What then is to be done? The answer, I believe, is neither more law, nor a legalistic pseudo-gospel of our own devising. The answer, even here and now, must be the gospel, the real gospel, God's own gospel: God's forgiveness and unconditional recognition. This means that *Christians*, as this gospel's bearers, have a unique social role to play. I shall comment on this role more extensively in the course of the following discussion. The overarching issue I hope to shed some light on is how the gospel brings about liberation from the debilitating captivity to the law, while at the same time staving off apparent lawlessness, not by adding more law but by giving human life a godly form. This is the first question to which we must address ourselves: What does it mean for humans to be impacted by the gospel and as Christians to be decisively shaped by it? What may come as a surprise here is that the law, as we shall see, is not simply left behind in the Christian life, but its energies are harnessed for the sake of the gospel. Then, as indicated earlier, I will ask, in light of my gospel emphasis, whether the Christian life can be captured by means of the law, that is, whether it can be given expression to, as well as encouraged, by the law. My skepticism in this regard will lead me to attempt a formulation of the Christian's attitude to the law.

The Gospel and the Law as God's Works

In discussing the impact of the gospel, we should, first, draw attention to the very nature of the gospel and, in particular, its distinction from law. With Luther, we have learned to distinguish sharply (though, in practice, rather haltingly) between the law and the gospel. "If we could only put an even greater distance between them!" Luther exclaims in his *Great Galatians Commentary*. The apostle Peter at Antioch is, for Luther, *the* exemplar of law-gospel confusion, wrongly "persuad[ing] believers they had to be justified by the Gospel and the Law *together*." A fatal mistake. Fatal, that is, for the gospel. For, if the law and the gospel are put on the same plane, it is the gospel that dies. The distinction, therefore, between the law and the gospel is there fundamentally for the gospel's sake. It underscores that the gospel is never something that is ours by right, something that God owes us by his very nature, something that we can take for granted, something proper to us, or something easy that we must put to work. In the course of his career, Luther dealt with a host of issues and a host of opponents. Yet underlying all of his polemic is this singular concern for the gospel. The gospel should remain gospel: it should always stand over against us as God's gracious promise to a guilty and condemned sinner. This promise is never a given; we never simply take it into ourselves and move on. Rather, time and again — by a sheer miracle — the gospel takes us out of ourselves, even as time and again we stubbornly return to a preoccupation with ourselves. The gospel — repeatedly! — makes saints. But it does so — out of sinners. It does this alone.

The antinomian controversy in early Lutheranism and Luther's polemic with Karlstadt both show, in different ways, what happens when the gospel is turned into something we can safely ascribe to ourselves and bless ourselves with. In the 1528 *Instructions* for the Saxony-wide visitation of parish pastors, Melanchthon defends the continued need for applying the law to Christians. "Many [preachers]," he writes, "now talk about the forgiveness of sins and say little or nothing about repentance." This leads people to "become[e] secure and without compunction of conscience.... We have admonished them to exhort the people diligently and frequently to repent and grieve over their sins and to fear the judgment of God." Then, almost in passing, Melanchthon adds an injunction which I consider to be quite significant: "The preachers are to condemn the gross sins of the common man, but *more rigorously* demand repentance where there is *false holiness*." It is the rise of this false holiness that is quite interesting. Melanchthon suggests that preaching merely the gospel leads not to moral laxity, as we might expect, but to "hypocritical holiness," like that of the Pharisees. Where the gospel does not come as a miraculous answer to an all-shattering accusation, where it is simply a given, it spawns a spirituality. In other words, where the gospel is allowed to be taken for granted, the gospel is crowded out and transformed into ... law. The gospel becomes commandment. This ought to give us pause. Another way in which the same destructive transformation happens is illustrated by the case of Karlstadt. Luther's polemic against his former colleague is a forceful defense of the objective, external character of the gospel. Luther warns that when one "tears down the bridge, the path, the way, the ladder, and all the means by which the Spirit might come," when "the outward order of God in the material sign of baptism and the oral proclamation of the Word of God" is absent — then the question is no longer "how the Spirit comes to you but how you come to the Spirit."

The antinomian controversy was a defense of the accusatory function of the law for the sake of the gospel; Luther's polemic against Karlstadt was a defense of the objective vehicles of the gospel. The preaching of the law in its accusing function *subjectively*, and the *objective* means through which the gospel stands over against me, both assure that the gospel does not become an entitlement but remains a sheer miracle of God's grace, ever new and ever miraculous, living water to a parched throat. By contrast, when the gospel is taken for granted, when one has a right to it, one must constantly assure oneself that that is still the case, that it can, in fact, be taken for granted. When all one has to go on is one's identity as a Christian, this inner conviction becomes true only if one's Christian identity can be externalized both for oneself and for others to see. One must authenticate it through a spiritual posture: the more rigorous, the more certain. One must show that one indeed is oneself. Thus one may choose to follow Jesus so radically that the particularity of his life becomes splintered into general examples to be emulated, regardless of whether there is a corresponding command. Or out of one's "spiritual and scriptureless brain," as Luther puts it, one may devise a self-chosen humility. Either way, says Luther, "the devil makes a commandment out of a promise of Christ and in place of faith institutes a human work."

The upshot of the antinomian controversy was the clarifying point that the gospel and the law work together, but do so on radically different planes. The law always accuses, so as to make one despair of oneself. The gospel then comes as good news, time and again assuring one of God's gracious favor and unmerited gifts. The gospel performs this task of rescue precisely in the context of the law's *ongoing* accusation. Now, for Christians specifically, the law's accusation aims at the temptation to see the gospel not as deliverance but as something natural and obvious, something domesticated that is in our bloodstream. Christians, in other words, are tempted to take the gospel for granted, and then to turn it into a challenge for themselves, a righteousness that gives shape to the gospel, to which, after all, they have every right. Living up to this challenge provides one (and everyone else) with tangible assurance of indeed having the gospel. But when the gospel is thus transformed into law, it becomes no different from the spurious gospels that society blesses itself with. It is no longer a miracle of God's coming. It turns into a message of self-discovery, of being yourself, of doing what is already in you (*facere quod in se est!*). It turns into a message and a task of authenticity.

This task acquires the urgency of a final solution. If I can and, indeed, must be myself … so surely can others! They, too, can and, indeed, must be themselves. And by being so, they can give a stamp of approval to my self-justification. My pathway to self-fulfillment becomes the way of universal salvation. This presumption, together with the need for approval underlying it, makes it into an act of godlessness. All hypocrites, Luther charges, "arrogate to themselves the divinity of Christ and His function. In fact, then, they do say: 'I am Christ, I am the Savior — not only *my own* but *for others* as well." But for all its hubristic pretense, this salvation can only be one spirituality among many. For when all is said, though not all is done, the holiness it puts forth is of exactly the same kind as those it considers deficient, lawless, and false. It, too, turns one into a "reckless worker," to use Luther's phrase, and ultimately sends one with a vengeance down the path of self-making and self-deception. That which was meant only to *justify the gospel* now relentlessly forces one to *justify oneself*. To come back to the law, then: in the case of Christians, the law accuses, always accuses (*lex semper accusat*) to keep one from making the foolish mistake of seeking to manipulate both the gospel and the law. No human can toy with the law without being overpowered and destroyed by it. By accusing, the law bares its teeth, so to speak, to show that it is not a plaything. Briefly put, neither the law nor the gospel can be domesticated and exploited for our own purposes. Both fundamentally remain God's realities and God's work.

In face of the law's accusation, the gospel brings comfort to the sinner and no one else but a sinner overcome by his own manipulativeness. The gospel assures the sinner of God's gracious acceptance and unmerited gifts. The gospel is that which catches the sinner running away from the law and from himself in exasperation and despair. But the gospel is not a safety net one can count on when things go wrong. It is always, time and again, a miracle, a Sabbath rest, a fatherly embrace when by all sober accounts there was only a precipice awaiting one over the hill. The gospel is a message of undeserved forgiveness for one who wanted to save himself and who also presumed to know how others ought to be saved. The gospel is a message of forgiveness for a would-be god. When it is believed, it brings peace to the conscience and cancels it. The gospel alone is God's final Word.

The Gospel as the Christian Life's Godly Form

In his discussion of the effects of the gospel, Luther emphasizes two things. First, we are radically distanced from ourselves, from our life in the law. We enter Christ's bridal chamber and shut all the world out, including our entire fleshly life up to this point and even from now on. I am, writes Luther, "pulled out of my own skin, and transferred into Christ and into His kingdom, which is a kingdom of grace, righteousness, peace, joy, life, salvation, and eternal glory." Second, we are also showered with gifts. As Christ takes upon himself our sin and our death, we become joined to him by "the wedding ring of faith" and receive his entire person: "faith ... takes hold of Christ the Savior Himself and possesses Him in the heart. Among the gifts bestowed on us are, in Luther's own words, Christ's "life, in which he swallowed up death; his righteousness, by which he blotted out sin; and his salvation, with which he overcame everlasting damnation. A poor man, dead in sin and consigned to hell, can hear nothing more comforting than this precious and tender message about Christ; from the bottom of his heart he must laugh and be glad over it."

Now, this distance to self and marriage to Christ have tremendous *practical* implications. In unpacking those, Luther draws on certain strands of medieval mysticism, especially the tradition associated with the *Theologia Germanica*. The *Theologia* criticizes what it calls "imagined detachment" and the desire to be "untouched by creaturely life ... not dependent on anything in this world, just like God in eternity." Its ideal is rather that of what it calls the "Christ-life," a life free from the self and lived for the sake of the Good. Its goal is true *obedience*, neither out of fear, nor for the sake of reward. "Christ's humanity," the *Theologia* declares, "was nothing but a house or habitation for God." To such a life, we, too, are called. Luther develops this theme of a life-in-Christ active in the world in *The Freedom of a Christian*. There, appealing to Philippians 2, he describes the Christian as a two-nature being: we are *divinized* through the communication of Christ's life, his concrete life and, therefore, like Christ, are now able to *descend* into and put on the neighbor with his needs and with his sins. With Christ being our very nature, we can now put on the neighbor's humanity. Christians become Christs to others, in order to share with them their righteousness, to liberate and to transform.

Two things are important to note here: First, with their lives hidden with Christ in God, to invoke another biblical image of Christian identity (Col. 3:3), Christians are infinitely more than they could ever make of themselves. They are "heavenly beings." They are thus freed from preoccupation with themselves, with their own being, or their own self-justification. Second, from their vital mooring in Christ, Christians also gain a different and hitherto impossible perspective on themselves. They now clearly perceive the destructiveness and futility of existence in the law. Specifically, with their lives hidden with Christ in God, Christians are distanced from the law and thus, for the first time, able to see not the performance of the law but the *neighbor* as the *ultimate* and *final* goal. They can see the neighbor in all his or her individuality as a desperate sinner or a fellow brother or sister in Christ.

We can hardly over-estimate the importance of this singular focus on the neighbor, as the Christian now descends into the world of law. The Christian, even as he or she reenters the world's structures, is actually able to see the law — all law: formal and unwritten — from a critical distance. This involves not only awareness that the law, as such, turns people into hypocrites, fuels their self-justification, and reduces them to their own works. Included here is also the insight that, by observing the law and nothing but the law, one may, in fact, do great *injustice* to the neighbor. For Luther, a case in point was the harshness with which some peasants were treated in the wake of the Peasants' Revolt. Some had been caught up in the events against their will; yet they had received the same punishment as the willful rebels. "If we do not make exceptions," Luther insisted, "and strictly follow the law we do the greatest injustice of all." For Luther, "all laws that regulate men's actions must be subject to justice, their mistress, because of the innumerable and varied circumstances which no one can anticipate or set down." Though Luther recognizes justice, or equity, to be a concept belonging to legal theory, he also insists that only Christians, as those who have no need to justify themselves and are thus free from the law, are able to practice justice in a consistent and unselfconscious manner. To make an exception, one must be able to see the sinner as an individual and as a neighbor. Only Christians are able to love the neighbor, before forming a judgment through the lens of the law.

The Peasants' Revolt may have been a bit of an exceptional situation for Luther. Elsewhere he maintains with far less reflectiveness that "[i]n society, obedience to the law must be strictly required" and sincerely believes this will prevent further rebellion, as long as the princes, too, treat their subjects justly. Still, his insight about the potential for injustice lurking in *every* social order is the one to emphasize. For us, it must be viewed against the backdrop of Zygmunt Bauman's brilliant analysis of the Holocaust: not, indeed, as a product of anti-Semitic sentiment, but of the perfectly well-functioning modern state. Bauman challenges the widespread assumption that "moral behavior is born of the operation of society and maintained by the operation of societal institutions, that society is essentially a humanizing, moralizing device and that, accordingly, the incidence of immoral conduct on anything more than a marginal scale may be explained only as an effect of the malfunctioning of 'normal' social arrangements." Bauman draws attention to a variety of aspects of the modern state that made the Holocaust possible. He points to rationalization of behavior in terms of costs and effects, which rules out opposition on rational grounds, the state's emphasis on efficiency, excellence and loyalty in the performance of duty, moralization of technology in such a way that only ends but not means are subject to moral evaluation, the state's diffusion of responsibility characteristic of all organizations, production of social distance, both in actual terms (which means that our actions can have an impact on those we will never encounter face to face) and in psychological terms (by deferring to expert knowledge). All these, Bauman argues, produce immoral behavior in otherwise perfectly moral, caring and loving people. To be able to resist this influence, the moral impulse must come from elsewhere. "Morality," Bauman concludes, "is not a product of society. Morality is something society manipulates — exploits, re-directs, jams." In light of

Bauman's critique of the modern bureaucratic society, one must agree with Luther that the fault always lies with the person; but one cannot agree that it never also lies with the office. This makes Christian's critical participation in the legal structures of society all the more necessary.

Bauman appeals to Emmanuel Levinas to argue that "responsibility is the essential, primary and fundamental structure of subjectivity ... morality is the primary structure of intersubjective relation." In other words, morality is a basic fact of our humanness; it arises as, conscious of another, we also become aware of ourselves. My relation to another thus logically precedes all formal structures, order, or laws. Bauman also shows how easily this focus on the neighbor is diverted onto the structure itself, within which we must make it, prove ourselves, justify our existence, and be ourselves according to a rigorous standard of what that means. We may, of course, try to manipulate this structure but, in reality, it is the structure that manipulates us: to be sure, it may curb our sinful desires, but it will also suppress our moral self for the sake of loyalty to itself. This destruction of the moral self is, in fact, inevitable, if it is indeed the case that we are all, even the apparent cultural antinomians, in thrall to a debilitating and oppressive undertow of law that characterizes human existence. And in this sense the psalmist is surely right when he says, "there is none who does good" (Ps. 14:1).

Luther's important insight in this context is that the moral subject truly arises only when Christ intervenes between me and my existence in the law, when, as Eberhard Jüngel puts it, I am "elementally interrupted" and become a person separate from my works. The moral *doer*, the doer of good works, must be raised to life first, outside of the law, in order then to descend into the world's law and in its midst to do good works. "A doer," Luther insists, "does not get this name on the basis of works that have been performed; he gets it on the basis of works that are to be performed. For Christians do not become righteous by doing righteous works; but once they have been justified by faith in Christ, they do righteous works." Sometimes the

Christian's works will accord with the specific law structure; at other times they will oppose it. But all the time the doer's focus will be not on the law but singularly on the neighbor. It is this insight — that the Christian as a doer comes before the law — that Luther expresses when he insists that Christians "do of their own accord much more than all laws and teachings can demand." In other words, they do it before such demand is even issued. This is the case because Christian obedience follows not the letter of the law, but flows from the christological structure of the doer's being. By his incarnation, Christ defines decisively what it means to be human, and he does so for all of us. Thus Christians — as Christs to the neighbor — are able to act in situations, or take into account circumstances, which the law has not foreseen, or provided for in detail. Christians can do so with loving sensitivity, especially toward the neighbor in bondage. This is what it means to live out of the gospel.

The Christian Life: Gospel or Law?

Before we ask whether Christian obedience can at all be captured and encouraged by means of the law, let me recapitulate the two mains points of the argument so far. First of all, I have argued for the necessity of maintaining the law's accusatory function, a function that is not only made explicit in preaching but, importantly enough, remains implicit in the inescapability of public judgment that attends human existence. Maintaining this accusatory function of the law remains of special significance for Christians, insofar as through an attitude of ownership toward the gospel they may exhibit a practical tendency toward antinomianism. What goes by the name of antinomianism is, at bottom, a tendency to turn the gospel into law in such a way that the law is no longer God's prerogative but one's own. Antinomianism thus not only destroys the gospel, as a work and gift of God, but transforms God's law into a project of personal and also public spirituality. So spiritualized, the law not only becomes a message of authenticity but as such comes to be viewed as the "gospel" and the panacea for the ills *du jour*. Precisely here one meets one's Waterloo. For no would-be god can toy with the law without eventually being crushed by its inexorable demand for self-justification. But at that point there no longer is any gospel to come to the rescue. At best, some alternative message of being oneself and doing all one can; at worst, inescapable judgment and a reverberating death sentence.

Over against this Christian temptation to underestimate the gift and play savior, I have stressed that neither the law, nor, more importantly, the gospel combined with law defines the Christian. The gospel alone does, with decisiveness and finality. In Luther's words, "a Christian, properly defined, is free of all laws and is subject to nothing, internally or externally.... For the Christian ... the entire law has been abrogated — whether it be the Ceremonial Law or the Decalog — because he has died to it." However, because of the temptation to take the gospel for granted and the law for a plaything, the law is not simply left behind. Rather, its consuming energies are harnessed by the gospel for the gospel's own sake: "the law does nothing but accuse consciences and manifest sin." Through its accusation, the law shows itself to be God's work, a tool that humans cannot wield without wreaking damage to their own and others' selves. More importantly, the law's accusation shows the gospel to be God's astonishing work and unmerited gift to a Christian constantly tempted to take the reins into his own hands and to bestow authenticity and power on the gospel one thinks one owns. In this way, in the face of the law's relentless indictment, the gospel remains a message of freedom from the law. The gospel remains God's final Word.

Second, in addition to the law's accusatory nature, I have insisted, following Luther, on the strongly ontological impact of the gospel on the believer. Christians live as accused sinners, ever anew and every graciously, being raised to a new life with Christ. The Christ-life involves both a personal and inter-personal transformation. As Luther puts it, "I do indeed live in the flesh, but I do not live on the basis of my own self"; rather, "this life ... is the life of Christ, the Son of God, whom the Christian possesses by faith." My life becomes "a mask of life" hiding Christ, who lives in me. Because the gospel is for the

Christian God's final Word, the sheer miracle of a new life, Christian existence embodies not the question, "How can I now be myself?," or, even worse, "How must I now be myself?" — as if the gospel were cheap, easy, and one's by right. Instead of the question, "How can and must I now be myself?," the question that the Christian life embodies is rather "For whose sake — for *whose* sake! — am I this new person-in-Christ?" That this is, indeed, the question which defines the Christian's active life is not only a corollary of the safe haven from the law's accusation which the gospel provides, a consequence of being rescued from preoccupation with the self. Concern with the neighbor is actually embodied in the Christian's personal being. The Christian life, like Christ's own concrete life, is a life of descent into the neighbor, of putting on the neighbor with his or her anxieties, enslavements, and sins. It is a life of first justifying the neighbor as a person before judging the neighbor's works.

The Christian life is thus characterized by freedom and obedience that both flow from the gospel. The law's role in the Christian life is quite circumscribed: rather than being left to itself and allowed to fuel human delusions of grandeur, the law assures that the gospel remains gospel, but as such the law does not define the Christian life. The law's function, to put it differently, is only to point away from itself — more than that, to drive the Christian away from the law — and toward the gospel. The gospel, as God's conclusive and final Word, provides a solution to the law's bondage, which characterizes all human existence; at the same time, it gives human life a *godly*, Christ-filled and Christ-like, form. For believers, the gospel is the Word of their being who has come to his own people and now dwells in our midst (cf., Jn. 1:11, 14).

To put things this way raises the question of the law's so-called third, pedagogical, use. This question of its development, definition, and reception is a complicated one from an historical perspective. I shall limit myself only to a few comments on Article VI of the *Formula of Concord* (1577). On the one hand, the *Formula*'s conception of the third use incorporates the former antinomian concern that the accusation of the law should be preached not only to unbelievers but also to Christians. The law's accusation aims at the desires of the flesh (§§ 9, 14). Beyond that, it is also directed at false holiness. It thus prevents Christians from devising their own law (§ 20) and drives home to them the imperfection and impurity of those works that happen to follow the divine law (§ 21). In this aspect, the *Formula*'s third use of the law is simply a reiteration of the law's accusatory function, with the explicit proviso that it applies to Christians, too. On the other hand, there are other concerns that the authors of the *Formula* seek to do justice to with their emphasis on instruction in the law. The first has to do with motivation. While Christians are said to perform works of the law spontaneously, "through the prompting and impulse of the Holy Spirit" (§ 2), the *Formula* repeatedly emphasizes that "the old creature still continues to hang on in their nature" (§ 7; cf. 18, 24). The spontaneity, properly characteristic of Christians, is thus stifled, and the resulting laxity can only be overcome through the law's "teaching, admonition, exhortation, [and] prodding" (§ 6). The second, even more important concern has to do with the content of Christian obedience. The *Formula*'s authors talk about the presence of the Holy Spirit in Christians and the empowerment that comes from the gospel (§ 11), but it is the law that gives shape to this otherwise naked and formless energy (§ 12).

What is absent from the *Formula*'s discussion of the law is any notion of the gospel's ontological impact beyond the presence of the Holy Spirit in the believer. The *Formula*'s blindness to the christological renewal of the Christian is one reason for its turn to the law in search of a rationale for, and structure of, Christian obedience. But this move is not without serious consequences. To begin with, resorting to the law on account of its motivational capacity calls into question the power and impact of the gospel. The law is brought in because, as it turns out, the gospel is unable to touch one's entire being, part of which must now be admonished and prodded by means of the law. The underlying assumption in the *Formula* is that, as a Christian, one is *partially* a saint and partially a sinner. This is quite different from the assumption operative in the argument we have advanced, namely, that one is *totally* a saint and totally a sinner. Hence the law must be directed at the entire person, even the Christian in the proper sense, so that the entire person might continually be embraced and defined by the gospel. The law does its work for the sake of the gospel being *gospel*, which alone decisively empowers and structures the Christian life. The law is not used to provide a temporary fix where the gospel falls short. Alongside of the power and impact of the gospel, the formula thus undermines the accusatory function of the law. While there is an intimation that self-devised spirituality might be the real problem, the *Formula* chooses, instead, to target spiritual laxity and ignorance. It, therefore, remains blind to the real issue, namely, the inescapable human compulsion toward self-justification, a compulsion that may even spawn a holiness that seeks to authenticate the naturalized gospel through a strict observance of God's law. This compulsion can only be brought to light through the law's uncompromising accusation. From this compulsion not the law but the gospel alone can save.

The *Formula*'s evisceration of both the power of the gospel and the accusing function of the law for the gospel's sake culminates in the *Formula*'s portrayal of the law as exhaustive of the Christian's active life. Sin, in the Christian life, is now only that which opposes God's law (§ 13). In light of our discussion, this must be seen as a significant blind spot that fails to take into account the Christian's temptation to seek self-recognition also in terms of divine law and to grant recognition to others on the law's terms. Consequently, the *Formula* endows the law with a finality that only the gospel can have. It repeatedly speaks of the law as God's immutable and unchanging will: "the word 'law' has one single meaning, namely, the unchanging will of God, according to which human beings are to conduct themselves in this life" (§15, cf. 3, 17). Not the interpersonal dimension preceding the law, but the law itself, becomes the form of the Christian's active life.

Over against the *Formula*'s position, I have shied away from granting the law the ultimacy and finality that by its very nature and our salvific presumption it strives to have. I shall address the proper attitude of the Christian, as one defined by the gospel, toward the law presently, as well as providing an example of the consequences of Christian self-justification through God's law. What remains for us to consider is the New Testament language that gives expression to the Christian life through imperatives. What about New Testament parenesis (e.g., Rom. 13–15; 1 Thess. 5)? What do we do with the so-called catalogues of virtues? Christians are told, for example, to think about praiseworthy things (Phil 4:8), to supplement their faith with virtue, to be self-controlled, steadfast, godly, full of brotherly affection (2 Pt. 1:5ff). Finally, Luther, too, opined that "the active life should be sought from the *Law*, which does not grasp Christ but exercises itself in works of love toward one's neighbor."

It seems to me one ought to see those sorts of injunctions in the same way one would view the gospel as a story. Both have the form they have on account of the limitations of discourse. And because of this form, both require the non-discursive operation of the Spirit. In the gospel's case, it is not the words that save but the Holy Spirit coming with them and "creat[ing] faith where and when it pleases God." Likewise, the apostolic encouragement is only a shadow of the outpouring of the Spirit on all flesh (Acts 2:17ff). The gospel without the Spirit becomes information, incredible information at that; the gospel form of life — the Christ-life — without the Spirit is only command. As such, it is both too little and too much. It is too much, in that, when it comes in the form of command, encouragement is inescapably also an accusation. It is too little, in that there is more to a rich, interpersonal relationship than the law can discursively provide for. Love is ultimately beyond legislation. However, that is how one can convey the gospel life in discourse. The Holy Spirit, on the other hand, conveys himself. In all, extensive exhortation and the catalogues of virtues notwithstanding, I agree with William Lazareth's view that "the biblically congruent climax of Luther's theological ethic is better expressed by God's gospel than by the law." For this reason, Lazareth prefers to speak of "the second or parenetic use of the Gospel," in addition to the first or salvific use. A command is only a shadow of the Christ-life that Christians lead, and it is not in it that Christians must ultimately seek their identity.

The Gospel as Critique of the Law

How then is the Christian to view the law, not only as one distanced from it but also as "lord of the Law" in its very midst? How are Christians to approach the law, even God's law, given that it is in its false independence and expansiveness that the law seeks to establish itself as the ultimate, the final word, the be-all-and-end-all of being and thus the way to salvation. What is there in the law for Christians if the law lacks this finality?

I have repeatedly stressed the law's accusation as underlying the Christian's being-in-the-gospel. But I also have noted, as a corollary of the Christian's freedom from the law and unconditional focus on the neighbor, that *all* order has the inherent potential for demoralizing, insofar as no law, however just, is ultimately able to produce a moral person. At best — if it is indeed just — the order has the capacity to extract moral behavior. But no law does away with human self-seeking or human hypocrisy. That is why no order or office can become a substitute for the presence of Christians, indeed of the Christian community, within it. When the order is apparently antinomian, the Christian has every right to criticize and oppose it. But whether it is the law of apparent lawlessness, or God's own law, the Christian is, above all, called to challenge the expansiveness of all law structures and their posturing, in our hands, to become final solutions. The Christian does so for the sake of the neighbor hopelessly mired in the law. Where necessary the Christian uncovers the coerciveness of those structures and thus puts the law in service to the gospel. The Christian brings out the law's accusation. At other times, all that may be needed is the message of gospel freedom. Whether the law is unjust or God's own, the point is to distance the sinner from the law, for the sake of the sinner and for the sake of the law. The gospel opposes the legalism of the law, its delusions of grandeur, its wanting to be, in our hands, the ultimate truth of being.

The important thing to observe here is that even God's law thus loses its finality. It is not the source, or final paradigm, of being. Only the gospel is. Wolfhart Pannenberg has insisted on this provisional character of any legal order by drawing attention to the historical nature of God's revelation. Pannenberg writes: "from the future of God" — that is, as already partakers of God's coming eschatological kingdom — "we receive the command to regulate human life in community according to law, but the form that was at one time appropriate for this life cannot be permanently biding; for each situation it must be determined anew in terms of God's future." It must, ideally, be determined in terms of what best serves the gospel and its focus on the neighbor. Yet one must also understand that, in the end, no law can relieve one of personal, Christ-like responsibility for the neighbor. In much the same vein, Luther, too, viewed the Decalogue as having been given only to the Jews and binding on us only insofar as it corresponds to natural law. And, even where natural law might be at stake, Jesus informs us that "in the resurrection they neither marry nor are given in marriage, but are like angels in heaven" (Mt 22:30).

Now, what needs to be strongly emphasized is that none of this means that the gospel relativizes the law into anything-goism, that one is now free to make laws for oneself as one pleases. This fear of un-policed spirituality — of empowerment without constraints — underlies the *Formula*'s recourse to the law (as well as many present-day jeremiads). But the gospel does not authorize one to create a new order, a new law in which one can then justify oneself. Far from it. The gospel, to repeat it again, once and for all removes me from the law, from needing to justify oneself. The gospel puts an end to being oneself, and realizing one's being, in terms of the law. Further, the gospel justifies me on account of Christ and bestows on me, a sinner, a new being: Christ-being. If I now find myself in the law, I exist in it only as a person on behalf of others, living the Christ-life to liberate them from the law's tyranny. This may mean exercising the law through the Spirit, or opening up within a legal order new opportunities corresponding to the Christ life. Whatever the case may be, my hope is in Christ.

Let me illustrate what I mean by applying the gospel's critique of the law to a topic that has for some time been a matter of significant controversy all over the western world: marriage. Lutheranism, historically, has its share of blame here. Marriage, as I think we all understand it, is not a vehicle through which one simply justifies one's sex-drive. Now, Paul does speak of marriage as a solution to immoral temptation (Rom. 7:2). Luther, too, linked marriage to sexual appetite in his critique of clerical celibacy. Yet, despite this dimension, marriage is fundamentally not a vehicle of self-justification. In the *Small Catechism*, Luther mentions "spouse and children" as blessings which one receives "out of pure, fatherly, and divine goodness and mercy, without any merit or worthiness of mine at all." Thus marriage is one of the institutions to which some Christians find themselves called to exhibit the Christ life, that is, to uphold each other and to make Christians out of sinners who come into the world. Marriage, from a Christian perspective, is, to be sure, just like any structure of order; but it is more than that: it is a vocation. But it never becomes a thing for itself, or just for me.

Here, I believe, Lutherans failed rather miserably when we looked at things from a historical angle. They failed in working out what it might mean when a legal institution such as marriage comes within the province of the gospel. Let me explain. Diarmaid McCulloch has pointed out that prior to the Reformation there existed a variety of ways in which one could function in society. Marriage was only one of them. But there were other avenues available to people who preferred a celibate life in community or in solitude. Of course, the motivation for maintaining those avenues might well have been legalistic and self-serving. But the important thing to note is that they existed. What happened in the wake of the Reformation and Luther's critique of monasticism was that this range of options for social existence was limited to one. Not upheld, but actually narrowed down. The notion of marriage as a blessing and vocation thus became occluded, and marriage became endowed with a finality it had never had previously. It now became an institution through which one achieved social visibility and respectability. It became the thing to do; in fact, the only thing to do. Rather than a blessing and an opportunity for living out one's Christ-life, it became a matter of social salvation and law, a matter of justifying oneself and proving one's social adjustedness. It became a thing for me. What should have happened, of course, is that the other modes of social being should have remained open, as legitimate options, as an intimation that the Christ-life for the neighbors transcends any particular order, which can otherwise easily become a vehicle of self- and other-justification. What happened, instead, was that the possibility of accusation was undercut (after all, one was doing the right thing, the godly thing, the only thing to do), and the gospel, as God's act of justifying one's entire existence, was made irrelevant. Now, I am not saying that this theological failure is the only cause of the current state and public perception of marriage. But we live with the fallout of a situation in which marriage was allowed to become the ultimate, the only way, and was thus turned into a vehicle for self-justification and social salvation. And for some it still is.

Conclusion

What I have tried to show in this essay, simply put, is that the gospel — and the gospel alone — is the answer to human existence in the law, even to apparently lawless existence. The gospel grants true freedom. It frees me from the need to be myself and, instead, gives me a new self. By giving structure to my person, it bestows it also on my life. For it gives me my self-in-Christ, living the Christ-life for the sake of fellow sinners and fellow brothers and sisters in Christ. In this sense, the gospel is not lawless, or disobedient. But because its obedience is not that of the law — though it will discursively coincide with some law — it gives me the important freedom to criticize and transform laws and to address sinners in bondage to the law.

This godly form that the gospel gives to the Christian life is, in fact, a life formed by the self-communication of the triune God, a very different kind of life from law-centered spiritualities of human devising. When all is said and done, the fundamental truth is not that we live in the midst of God's immutable will to which we must conform but in the midst of the Father's gracious blessing — the blessing of a relationally rich life, lived in union with Christ and empowered by his Spirit.

A Resurrection Hermeneutic:
Law and Gospel in Preaching and Worship

Amy C. Schifrin

I

The warmth of the Apostolic Greeting, the joy of the Hymn of Praise, the stillness of time between Salutation and Collect, the fearless reading of the Word of God, the vibrant proclamation of the sermon, the deep thanksgiving of the offertory, the reverent bow at the Sanctus, the love outpoured at the Fraction, the tears during the Distribution, the deep peace at the Benediction.

All these things and many more happen in the course of a Eucharistic liturgy. We call this underlying grammar of Eucharistic liturgy within the yearly church calendar the *ordo*, and while we can see it on paper, it does not truly exist apart from its enfleshment in the Christian assembly, for these words and acts are not simply random events strung together willy-nilly, but they are expressive of the Apostolic faith passed down through the scaffolding, or grammar of the liturgy that emerges in the earliest gatherings of the Christian church on earth.[1] In and through the liturgy we are given the scriptural Word in liturgical form, not simply to know what the Word of God means, but to receive and experience what the Word of God is doing to us and for us in this moment and forevermore. In the liturgy we

---

1. Preaching's roots are ever in the *ordo*, a structure inherited from Jesus' forbearers, for the gathering itself is an interpretation of the Word. Lathrop speaks of the assembly being like the "Bible alive." *Holy Things: A Liturgical Theology* (Minneapolis: Fortress Press, 1998), 15.

begin to live by every word that proceeds from the mouth of God, because in the liturgy, God is the subject and we are the object. He is the One acting upon us in holy love, reading our hearts and claiming us in a love that puts our death-dealing impulses to death and brings to life a new creation in Christ again and again. In the liturgy, those events by which salvation is given to the world, are given (in the eternal now of kairotic time) to us. We were not there when the earth was created; we were not there when the angels sang over Bethlehem; we were not there when Moses came down the Mount of Sinai with two tablets of law; we were not there when Jesus hung between earth and sky, between the heavens and a garbage heap, between time and eternity; we were not there, but in the Eucharistic liturgy, in Word proclaimed and Sacrament received, in prayer and hymn, in the depths of confession and the holy peace of absolution, in trinitarian invocation and benediction, we are brought *there* through the eternal love of God. "Join our prayers with those of your servants of every time and every place and unite them with the ceaseless petitions of our great High Priest until he comes as victorious Lord of all." Through him, with him, in him, all that is and all that is to come are given to us as he lifts our hearts in thanksgiving, in a Great Thanksgiving.

The broad topic today is applying law and gospel in preaching and worship, and from the outset it is important to note that Preaching and the Divine Liturgy are not two distinct or separate things, but one event, one event in which the whole is far greater than the isolated enactment of any of its parts. "The whole liturgy is sacramental."[2] Preaching, itself, is a form of worship whose home is in the Eucharistic liturgy.[3] Like, hymnody, its twin, it is a performative doxological exegesis of the Living Word of God. It is done to and for the glory of God, and its primary purpose is to bring the dead to life, to true life in Christ. When the inspired writers of the Holy Scripture

---

2. Alexander Schmemann, *For the Life of the World* (New York: St. Vladimir's Seminary Press, 1973), 42.

3. Geoffrey Wainwright, "Preaching as Worship," *The Greek Orthodox Theological Review* 28, no. 4 (Winter 1983), 325-336

penned those sacred words on stone, parchment, or papyrus, they did so not simply for people to read them in a book, but so the words would be sounded in an assembly, a worshiping congregation. They wrote those words down with power, salvific power still in them, and that power was intended to be released when the Word was sounded again. They heard the Word — the living voice of the living God — they were killed and made alive — and they did believe. Then, they wrote that Word down so that we would hear his Living Voice and believe as well. In preaching, the Divine voice continues to sound, for it is alive in the human voice, breaking down this shell of an autonomous individual body as it pierces and prevails all the way to our heart. It is from a human voice, a preacher's voice, that those who hear are included in the living story of God's love for all the world. As that gift of faith comes, it is death to our rebellion and joy to our fainting hearts. God's Word will accomplish its purpose and prosper in the thing for which he sent it (Is. 55): calling, gathering, and enlightening, forgiving, healing, and strengthening the assembly which is now caught up in the holy and spectacular love of God, Holy Father, Holy Son, and Holy Spirit.

Can this merciful word be preached apart from the Eucharistic liturgy, you ask? Of course, but it will not complete its purpose until our eyes are opened in the breaking of bread (Lk. 24:30-31).[4] And here is the caveat ... unless law and gospel are rightly distinguished in the preaching of the Word, our eyes may be opened, but our vision will be myopic. Unless the two-edged sword of the Word both kills and makes alive, the means by which God seeks to shower his mercy upon us (Word and Sacrament) will be thwarted, for our gathering will be misunderstood as our own doing, just as the improper distinction between Law and Gospel leads us to believe that salvation is also our own doing.

---

4. "It is now the liturgical function of the sermon to plant carefully in the hearts of the assembly the seeds of the gospel which has been proclaimed, so that when they approach the physical sign of the Word, the body and blood which are broken and spilled, they will recognize their Lord.... The assembly sees Christ in the Eucharist through the Word which has been preached to them." Timothy Clark, "The Function and Task of Liturgical Preaching," *St. Vladimir's Theological Quarterly*, no. 01 (2001), 44-45.

Early in the fifth century, Prosper of Aquitaine wrote, *ut legem credendi lex statuat supplicandix*.[5] (We often hear this in its shortened form, *lex orandi, lex credendi*). It means, in essence, that the law of praying establishes the law of believing, or as I like to frame it, as the church prays, so she believes. Prosper, in line with the witness of St. Augustine, wrote this to address the issue of semi-Pelagianism in the church, for the semi-Pelagians believed that the human had to make the first move towards salvation. It was a matter of free-will. Once a human being made that move, then God would give his grace (a conditional promise if I've ever heard one). Salvation depended upon our actions, so that we, rather than God, would come to wield the law to our own advantage. The law then was not something that came from God to us, as if without his grace we were capable of seeing the depth of our own sin,[6] as if we could remove our own sin without God putting the Old Adam or Eve in us to death. But when law and gospel are rightly parsed and given to us, we who are the object of God's love will experience the law's power to kill as it exposes our assumptions of autonomy and free-will. (Regardless of what Frank Sinatra says, you cannot do it your way.) The unanimity in form and content of preaching and praying within the weekly eucharistic celebration of our Lord's victory over sin and death becomes crucial to the shaping of our faith, so that we do not go astray and turn gospel into a new law, a new demand, i.e., you must first ask God to save you before he will act on your behalf. Prosper is looking back to 1 Tim. 2:1-6, to the command to pray (i.e., that supplications be made), and sees that is not without a unified content and grammar. For as Timothy urges a multiplicity of prayer forms within the liturgical structure "supplications, prayers, intercessions, and thanksgivings be made for all men," so the center of this structure is given us by the one Mediator between God and man, the one Mediator who is still praying without ceasing, who is still present when his Word is proclaimed,

---

5. *Capitulum* 8, PL 51, "so that the law of praying establishes the law of believing" or "let the rule of belief be established by the rule of prayer."

6. This is like telling the dentist with drill poised over my mouth to route out decay, "Just hand me the drill, I'll do it myself."

and who is with us as he is placed in our hands and we hear the sweetest of words, "The Body of Christ given for you." He is here where he has promised to be because the most High and Holy God wants all men to be saved. He is here with angels and arch-angels, surrounding us with cherubim and seraphim. He calls us to experience his divine life in word, song, and gesture; in, with, and under earthly elements and the speaking of promises remembered. If we can call the liturgy the church's work in any sense, here is a work that is a pure gift to perform, for in Christ Jesus we are joined to the heavenly liturgy. The source and destination of our supplications is God, our Father and it is in his only begotten Son that the law is fulfilled (Mt. 5:17), and it is in and through his Holy Son that the church is brought to prayer (Heb. 2:17-18). As the church prays, so she believes.

Prosper's declaration that the rule of prayer establishes the rule of belief expresses what sacramental worship is and does implicitly, for we do not gather on our own but are called into this life of prayer in the assembly of the faithful, in the verity of Apostolic witness, by the breath of the Holy Spirit. Dead in our own sin, our prayers are never the first move in our salvation. We do not create our prayers or our faith *ex nihilo* but they are breathed into us by the One whose sighs are always deeper than words, by the One who is already and ever-praying for us without end, by the One who is the author and giver of all our lives, by the One who is One, Father, Son, and Holy Spirit. The Holy Trinity is present in every page of Scripture, and the liturgy is the place in which the Scripture comes to us in such a way that it works its goodness through us as one by one we are made into the body of Christ. We are moved into the life of faith by God himself, for we are brought into the love of the Holy Trinity through Christ our Lord, the One who teaches us to pray, the One who, on the night of his betrayal gives us his body, the One who carries the weight of our rebellion as thorns pierce his brow, the One, who when lifted high on the cross, stretches out his hands to draw all men to himself.

Three days later, in the Eucharistic liturgy of the Emmaus Road, the Risen Jesus takes bread and blesses it. *Baruch Ata*

Adonai, Eloheinu melech ha olam ha motzee lechem min ha-aretz. Amen.[7] He breaks it and gives it to us to eat. If within our Eucharistic liturgies the preaching of the Word, both law and gospel have occurred, so that we are flayed open, hearts now exposed, looking to God for our very breath, then our lives as the church, as the body of Christ, will be sacramental in that we live in unity with him, as vessels of his love for all the world. Then we can tell the story as it was meant to be told. When joy becomes the care of the neighbor, when in sacrifice we feel no loss but only love, when we are so overwhelmed by the mercy of God that there is nothing, absolutely nothing to do but to give thanks, then the Word will have had his way with us. Preaching and Eucharist are but a single Word, the Living Word who draws us into his life by his sacrifice, and through his life into the full embrace of the Holy Trinity.

II

Gospel is turned into law when we have to first *do* something. When we are called to trust in our own decision over against the power of God to save, it is implicit that anyone who has not made such a decision is thought to be less deserving than we are. Unfortunately, there are no safeguards where humans are involved, so the preaching of law is misused and mis-understood when the semi-Pelagians in every generation demand that others make the first move towards faith. Some preachers will bludgeon a congregation with their words: You *should* do this. You *ought* to do that. You *must* believe. They think they are preaching the law in calling their congregations to repentance or to an amendment of life, but in fact they are simply calling them to be the subject rather than the object of the law. They are clueless as to the function and theological intent of the law, and truly uninformed as to the performative power of a spoken word. Even cloaked in Lutheran language, someone might really be asking you to pray a "Sinner's Prayer" and to accept Jesus into your heart. (That's all you have to do, to get your life

---

7. Blessed art thou, O LORD, our God, King of the universe who brings forth bread from the earth.

on track. That's all you have to do to have eternal life. Accept him.) In doing so they have flattened the salvific events given to us through the assembly's liturgical enactment, they have flattened a holy event into a prescribed formula. The law has not killed anyone here, because if it's your choice to believe, to accept, you are still in control.

Some of the problem comes from a poor reading of the text that contributes to a faulty hermeneutic. Sometimes folks think one passage of Scripture is only law and another only gospel.[8] Blessed are the meek. Law or Gospel? Don't ask first what it means, ask first what the words do. "Blessed are the meek" and the woman with the big bouffant hairdo in the pew says, "uh-oh," since she wouldn't be caught dead being meek, and she wouldn't want to be caught dead with someone who is meek. To her this word is law, and the Word spoken will slay her at the same time as it will speak mercy to one whose back is bowed low, whose belly is empty, whose bed is a cardboard box in the filth of a Calcutta street. Blessed are the meek is pure mercy to one who knows they need God just to breathe. The faulty hermeneutic is shallow reading. It looks only to the surface of the text, but Holy Scripture like every other liturgical text carries a thickness of meaning that is discovered and rediscovered only when it is given, sounded in our ears, within the context of prayer. In the liturgy, Scripture reflects on Scripture, and brings us to the center of a holy and faithful conversation between God and his people. A true law/gospel distinction can only be made manifest within this hermeneutic of trust, trust that even as we read, God is reading us. A superficial reading of Holy Scripture with a semi-Pelagian hermeneutic will turn Gospel into Law because when one isolates a text and makes it an

---

8. Luther declares that, "There is no word in the New Testament that does not look back to the Old, in which it was proclaimed before. The New Testament is nothing more than a revelation of the Old; just as when someone first had a sealed letter and then opened it. In like manner the Old Testament is a testamentary letter of Christ, which he opened after his death and had read and proclaimed everywhere through his gospel." *Sermon on Christmas Day on John 1:1ff., ChurchPostil*, 1522, WA 10 I, 1, 181:21ff. in Heinrich Bornkamm, *Luther and the Old Testament*, 2nd edition, trans. Eric W. and Ruth C. Gritsch (Mifflintown, PA: Sigler Press, 1997), 82.

item or a principle which we have the power to accept or reject, there is no place to experience that work which God is doing when his voice is sounding through ours in the assembly.

When we look at the major homiletic theories of the last hundred years, and take them apart seeking to see how they enhance or dismiss law/gospel distinctions, we find that much of what passed for common knowledge in the early 20th century and much of what passes for common homiletic knowledge or rhetorical technique or exegetical practice in the early 21st leads either to an inerrancy that only works when a law/gospel dialectic is exchanged for a propositional/persuasive free-will one or when it is exchanged for a deconstruction of the Apostolic witness that leads to a boundary-breaking lawlessness where one will inevitably worship the creature rather than the Creator.

With the former hermeneutic we get three points and a poem. Say a preacher interprets the text in a linear fashion, as if a parable was a scientific formula, in which assent to point A will lead to assent of point B, which will lead to point C, then a poem to illustrate the "proof," and then the hearer says, "Yes, I believe." Now I'm saved while surrounded by thousands, and this so-called personal relationship with Jesus is not only personal, it is private, because Jesus is in my heart. Such preaching is only possible if a human is believed to have a free-will in matters of salvation. It often relies on transmission of "information" about the Bible, using deductive techniques to transmit an objective truth. The goal of such preaching is to give hearers a definitive means by which to understand the physical and spiritual worlds that they inhabit.[9] Exegesis of the text has its own goal of formulating a preaching idea, exposition of the unchanging universal truth which is the remedy for all that ails

---

9. In preaching on the 90th Psalm at Second Baptist Church, St. Louis, M. Ashby Jones states, "Self-search for that underlying purpose of preaching seems to reveal that in one way or another I am always striving to give men a spiritual interpretation of the world in which they live." M. Ashby Jones, "Making the Word Flesh," in Joseph Fort Newton, *If I Had Only One Sermon to Prepare* (New York & London: Harper and Brothers Publishers, 1932), 57.

humankind.[10] This genre of traditionalist preaching wants to transmit the truth about God in such a way that people are persuaded to believe this truth, for in believing they will be saved. It simply tells people what to believe and why to believe it, and you can hear it all day long on popular Christian stations. The preacher has deduced some isolated thought from Scripture or from his/her observation of the world and turned it into a "preaching idea."[11]

Traditionalist preaching is attractive, even in many Lutheran circles, because upon first hearing it, it appears to uphold the authority of Scripture as it uses much of the same language as long-standing law/gospel preachers. However, it uses the language quite differently. Because such preaching primarily seeks to persuade or convince (rather than to kill and make alive), it has at its foundation some strand of that same semi-Pelagian heresy.[12] The hearer is called to embrace what is presented as a "scriptural worldview," and once it is embraced, they can apply the teachings they have received to every aspect of their lives. This preaching seeks to move the hearer from vice to virtue, or from virtue to an even greater virtue, so it is an easy sell. But when we examine closely how such preaching treats the Holy Scripture, we find that loosed from its moorings in the sacramental life of the church, it examines Scripture as a flat document without life-giving power. The power comes from the one who has faith, often a tall good-looking smooth-talking preacher (although sometimes it will be a woman in red high heels with

---

10. Paul Borden, "Is There Really One Big Idea in That Story," in *The Big Idea of Biblical Preaching: Connecting the Bible to People (In Honor of Haddon Robinson)* (Grand Rapids: Baker Books, 1998), 67-80.

11. "[Jesus'] purpose seemed, not to reveal new things to men, but rather to reveal familiar things in a new light." Newton, 60. As Haddon Robinson defines what an idea is, "An idea begins in the mind when things ordinarily separated come together to form a unity that either did not exist before or *was not previously recognized*" (italics mine). Haddon W. Robinson, *Biblical Preaching: The Development and Delivery of Expository Messages* (Grand Rapids, Michigan: Baker Academic, 1980, 2001), 39. According to this train of thought, Jesus may have come to give us new ideas with which "we make sense out of the parts of our experience." Robinson, *Biblical Preaching*, 39.

12. I.e., Arminianism.

big eye-lashes)[13] who has come upon a virtuous idea which he can then support with isolated Scripture passages, who will then state this divine objective "truth" in a propositional form that the hearer can grasp and affirm. This sort of exegesis that is done by playing scriptural roulette is not what Luther meant when he said that Scripture interprets Scripture.

One example of a such an erroneous hermeneutic is the handing out of a sheet of paper before the sermon that has both words and blank spaces to be filled in. On that sheet of paper the preacher has given the congregation a summary of the important points in his/her sermon, but with crucial words missing. If the people listen carefully enough, they can fill in the blank correctly (a good work) and then be able to transmit the information they've received from the preacher in another encounter. These short concrete ideas will then become the filter by which people approach the Holy Word during the week. Each of these sermons will serve to show how the application of some timeless scriptural truth will meet a present need,[14] and "secure a moral action."[15] Law becomes my law, and gospel will again become law when it must be accepted in this mechanistic way. Like "The Four Spiritual Laws" of Campus Crusade for Christ, your faith will rest on how well you accept the law.[16] The pattern of this "saving Law" becomes a new liturgy between individuals who would brazenly seek to save another apart from the church's gathering in word

---

13. In the late 19th Century Phillips Brooks coined the phrase, "Truth through personality" in which the gospel comes through the personality or attributes of the preacher. Transparency is not sought, but the hearer is understood to meet Jesus in the persona of the preacher. By the 21st century, that persona has grown to larger proportions with the onslaught of electronic media. See Philips Brooks, *Lectures on Preaching* (London: H.R. Allenson, Limited, 1877).

14. James Massey, "Hermeneutics for Preaching," in *Review and Expositor* 90, vol.3 (Summer 1993), 367.

15. "There is scarcely anything so dull and meaningless as Bible doctrine taught for its own sake.... Theological truth is useless until it is obeyed. The purpose behind all doctrine is to secure moral action." A.W. Tozer, *Of God and Men* (Harrisburg, PA: Christian Publications, 1960), 26-27; quoted in Robinson, *Biblical Preaching*, 107.

16. http://www.campuscrusade.com/fourlawseng.htm.

and sacrament, apart from water and wine, apart from the grammar of the *ordo* that seeks to bring us into an encounter, not just with a text, but with the Divine.

In reaction to what is falsely named a literal or inerrantist interpretation of Scripture,[17] there are those in the early twenty-first century church who will look to any place other than scripture to find their inspiration for preaching. They may not want to look as closely at textual details and certainly not at the particularities of the cross as much as they want to look for the principles they believe are presented in the Scriptures that match their current post-modern worldview. This worldview is often based on certain democratic, communal, and non-hierarchical principles.[18] It is a worldview in which there is an equality or a diversity of truths, with no one truth that should be forced upon another. Here, there is truth everywhere, so they say that it is neither the church's nor the preacher's work to impose the laws that order their own lives on anyone else.[19] Those laws you read about in the Bible, they don't apply to us, they say, "especially the ones in the Old Testament. They're culturally conditioned. We're not living in the fifth century B.C. We're not even living in the first century. We know more now about the human condition, the human body and psyche than those ancients did, and we need to listen now to enlightened, well-educated voices. Doesn't Scripture tell us to look for truth anywhere we can find it? Besides, we are not Jews, they say, we are Christians, and Christ is the end of the law. Scripture is again made into an object, but rather than simply an object from which to gain power, it is an object to dissect, and any privileged historic theology that was held in esteem by a previous group with a history of cultural power is to be dismantled.

---

17. Literalism is really a selective literalism. Inerrancy is simply a wooden reading of scripture from a free-will hermeneutic presented in a pseudo-scientific, "factual" way.

18. Lucy Atkinson Rose, *Sharing the Word: Preaching in the Roundtable Church* (Louisville: Westminster John Knox Press, 1997), 121-131.

19. Ann Kirkus Wetherilt, *Voices of Women: Echoes of God* (New York: Continuum, 1994), 95.

When one does look at the biblical text from such a lens, it is far more likely that one will preach the criticism of the text rather than the witness of the text.[20] Under the guise of "diversity," of inviting "all the voices to the table" (so that every odd and eccentric behavior known to humankind is given as much weight in interpreting the text as is the received text itself), they may privilege voices that have not been shaped by the salvific events that are recorded in the biblical text.[21] Such preachers may use a plethora of heartwarming stories (á la *Chicken Soup for the Soul*) so that the good feeling that comes from the poignant ending becomes a filter by which the biblical text is heard, and the particularities of law and gospel are subsumed under a generic principle of love. Finally, there are some whose hermeneutical guide is an anger born of a perceived sense of being victimized by the institutional church and they may seek to use the pulpit to set things right, to be on the side of "justice."

Unwittingly, the gospel, God's merciful love for all humankind, has been turned into just another law here. The language is further away from the old law/gospel dialectic, but the underlying grammar is no different than the inerrantist's, for they are still calling for an assent to a proposition. The proposition is just hiding in a more hip set of clothes, and the persuasion is far more subtle because it is aimed more at a person's emotions than at their logical thought processes. The interpretive error that leads to a polar opposite misread of the law/gospel distinction simply says that the law is no longer needed because Jesus is love. Jesus is presented here as the embodiment of a generic principle of love, rather than the second person of the Trinity. This generic love, devoid of the cross of Christ and his

---

20. "We must consider how to read and preach Scripture in such a way that opens up its message and both models and fosters trust in God. So much of the ideological critique that currently dominates the academy fails to foster these qualities. Scripture is critiqued but never interpreted. The critic exposes but never exposits. Thus the word itself recedes into the background, and we are left talking about the politics of interpretation, having lost the capacity to *perform* interpretations." Richard B. Hays, "Salvation by Trust? Reading the Bible Faithfully," *The Christian Century* 114, no. 7. (26 February 1997), 223.

21. Mary Donovan Turner and Mary Lin Hudson, *Saved from Silence: Finding Women's Voice in Preaching* (St. Louis: Chalice Press, 1999).

glorious resurrection, is incapable of creating the unity among peoples which it touts so proudly in myriad public and ecclesiastical venues, because the world is incapable of experiencing love as long as it is hell bent on its own way, incapable of a love that seeks the best for the neighbor until the law of God exposes one's sin, exposes that people love the darkness more than the light, exposes that people prefer to trust in their own judgment since truly, it's so much more manageable than the judgment of God (Heb. 4:12-13).

In some post-modern preaching, the preacher does not have any authoritative content to communicate, but is to help the hearers to find their own truths and to make their own meaning of the world.[22] But, where there is no law, neither is there gospel, for these preachers propose that people are capable of making their own decisions about what if any law to obey. It's a far more covert offer than three points and poem but it works the same way, for in the end, you are left with yourself, and there is no more dangerous god than any one of us. Like the flimsy generic products in the sale aisle of the discount house, the generic love that is offered here will simply fall apart before the day is out, and certainly will give you no comfort for the night that is coming.

III

Unlike preaching in which an individual's interpretation of his/her own experience becomes the highest authority, the sort of preaching that leaves the self in control of either personal "mo-

---

22. "The goal of ... any sermon, is to offer a vision of a particular aspect of Christian reality and Christian existence, a vision that is drawn from scripture (and ecclesial tradition) and is informed by critical forms of contemporary knowledge and experience, a vision that is concrete enough to be assimilated into the very being of the hearers. It is not important that hearers remember the content of any particular sermon, but that the sermon empower them to internalize the language and concepts of the faith in such a way that the language and concepts inform who they are, how they ascribe meaning to the world, and how they act and live in the world. To enable this sermons must be dialogical in nature...[which] means that preachers must not hand down absolute, authoritatively pronounced truths; they must offer invitations to the hearers to engage the vision of the sermon intellectually, emotionally, and experientially." O. Wesley Allen, *Preaching Resurrection* (St. Louis: Chalice Press, 2000), 5.

rality" or of communal "justice," preaching that truly puts sinners to death and raises up new persons in Christ understands that in every sermon there is a confrontation going on, an encounter with our crucified and risen Lord. Law/Gospel preaching does not simply tell about Jesus, for such preaching is not primarily about giving information.[23] It is not about the transmission of facts, but the mediation of the truth, of the One who is truth. In and through a preacher's words, Christ is coming to you, but since this world does not want to meet him, God uses the law to drive us to the place where we can at last see the magnitude of our sin, and then see his mercy, which is brighter than heavens. In the words of Gerhard Forde,

> the point of [the law/gospel] distinction is once again the making public of the divine deed, making it hearable in a world that will not hear it. The distinction is made so that a new kind of speaking might be heard in this world: gospel speaking.... Proclamation, shaped by the theology of the cross, is governed by the distinction between law and gospel. This distinction comprehends the fact that publication of the electing deed cannot proceed directly to the world that crucified Jesus, but must bring it to an end.[24]

Through the law, God drives us to the cross, and like the wind that rustles the leaves in our gardens, once we are unclothed, we have no place to hide. Preachers need not bring

---

23. The placement of every text within the ordo of the cultic meal reveals that Christ Jesus himself "gives to every text its interpretation...; he is the one who gives to every text its eternal content." Yngve Brilioth, trans. Karl E. Mattson, *A Brief History of Preaching* (Philadelphia: Fortress Press, 1965), 10.

24. Gerhard Forde, "Called and Ordained," in Todd Nichol and Marc Kolden, eds., *Lutheran Perspectives on the Office of Ministry* (Minneapolis: Fortress Press, 1990), 122, 128. Schmemann speaks a similar word from the realm of liturgical theology, "The world rejected Christ by killing him, and by doing so rejected its own destiny and fulfillment. Therefore if the basis for all Christian worship is the Incarnation, its true content is always the Cross and the resurrection. Through these events the new life in Christ, the Incarnate Lord, is 'hid with Christ in God,' and made into a life 'not of this world.' The world which rejected Christ must itself die in man if it is to become again means of communion, means of participation in the life which shone forth from the grave, in the kingdom which is not 'of this world,' and which in terms of this world is still to come." Schmemann, *For the Life of the World*, 122.

their hellfire and brimstone out of their back pockets because it's not their job to do the accusing. The law which exposes our mortality can do that all on its own, but the words of the preacher "identify the point where the law stands against the hearer."[25] We don't need to make the accusation but are called to simply point to it like a road sign that says, "Jerusalem, 20 miles." Like a mirror on the wall, law reflects fallen human existence back to us. But when the scales are still on our eyes, we cannot even see ourselves, so it takes an encounter (in our case, a ritual encounter) with Jesus whom we are persecuting (Acts 9:1-20). The true mirror of our fallen rebellious existence is the cross, the cross of Christ, hanging bloody. You can describe that cross day and night, but until it is your death, the death of all that keeps you bound to death, you will turn that mirror every which way but in. The law reveals that we are enemies of the cross, we are the persecutors of our Lord. Law/gospel preaching does not need to set out to make a person feel guilty and then offer them a cheap salve (all you have to do is_____). Law/gospel preaching, as the Word of our crucified and risen Lord, knows that we are guilty. Preaching that kills and makes alive brings the hearer before the Lord because in preaching that kills and makes alive, the Lord is fully present.

The work of the law never stands on its own, nor is it its own end. Every sermon we preach needs to have at its center what I call a resurrection hermeneutic: "If Christ has not been raised, then our preaching is in vain, and your faith is in vain" (I Cor. 15:14). Preaching is the announcement or heralding of God's truth through *human* speech. Or we could say that preaching is the saving Word of Scripture doxologically proclaimed. In law/gospel preaching a mediation occurs, a revelation occurs. Jesus says, "I am the bread of life...; I am the way, the truth and the life...; I am the resurrection and the life." Jesus is giving us the gift of eternal life.[26] When a Christian preacher preaches according to a law/gospel resurrection hermeneutic — whether

---

25. James Nestingen, "Preaching Repentance," in *Lutheran Quarterly*, Vol. 3, no.3 (Autumn 1989), 260.

26. Nestingen, "Preaching Repentance," 260.

he is preaching on the first commandment, or on the first breath of man, or on the fruit of the Spirit — he will be mediating the saving truth of Jesus Christ. For through the preacher the eternal mercy of God, now sounded in human speech, is putting an end to all the other little gods who seek to claim us. Law and gospel are given in a single breath, the Holy Breath of God who calls, gathers, enlightens, and makes holy the whole Christian church on earth.

It is overwhelming to think that the real presence of God can be heard through the human voice as surely as it can be placed in your hands — given and shed for you, and that the fulfillment of the kingdom, the fullness of the reign of God, the cosmic struggle between good and evil are being played out in the battlefield of your heart when the Word of God is spoken into your lives.[27] While we may speak of the Bible as Old Testament and New Testament, there is no time limit on the commandments of God. They fill the content of the New Testament as fully as they do the Old, announcing God's sovereignty over all that is and all that is to be. A law/gospel resurrection hermeneutic understands that the first commandment (and all the other commandments) are still sounded in the New Testament, but they are now sounded in an eschatological fullness through Jesus Christ, the ever-living Word, the One in whom the law is fulfilled.[28] The eternal presence of God, Father, Son, and Holy Spirit, was written into those tablets of law, "I am the Lord your God; I am who I am: I will be who I will be; I am the resurrection and the life; I am your resurrection

---

27. "One can speak of the 'real presence' of Christ in the readings of the scriptures in much the same way that some Christian traditions speak of Christ's real presence in holy communion...We can say that the reading of the scriptures in the liturgical assembly is sacramental in that it is an effective sign of the presence of Christ." William Skudlarek, *The Word in Worship: Preaching in a Liturgical Context* (Nashville: Abingdon, 1981), 88.

28. "Luther did not invent [the] relationship between Old and New Testament; rather, he read it out of the New Testament itself. He aptly observed how little Paul and Peter report the individual acts of Jesus in their letters: Paul wrote gospel by making mighty sermons out of a very few passages of the Old Testament, whose fulfillment in Christ he demonstrated." Heinrich Bornkamm, *Luther and the Old Testament*, 85.

and your life." Preachers who see that the Holy Trinity, one God, Father, Son, and Holy Spirit, is present in every page of Scripture will, in faith, announce what God has been doing all along in his great love for the world which he has made.[29] And when they do so, rightly parsing law and gospel through a resurrection hermeneutic, they will be eschatologically heralding the victory that is ours in Jesus Christ. Apart from the final victory in Christ, there is no way to rightly distinguish law from gospel, for from apart for the victory that is Christ's we would always be striving in vain to resurrect ourselves on our own.

In opposition to the world's preaching, of law masquerading as gospel, and of the church which has foolishly succumbed to it, I'd like to take you into a glimpse of the homiletic process of distinguishing law and gospel, and so I'd like you to think for a moment about a text that appears twice in the NRCL, once in Epiphany (6A) and then later in the Sundays after Pentecost (Proper 18c). The text is Deut. 30:15-20:

> [15]See, I have set before you today life and prosperity, death and adversity. [16]If you obey the commandments of the Lord your God that I am commanding you today, by loving the Lord your God, walking in his ways, and observing his commandments, decrees, and ordinances, then you shall live and become numerous, and the Lord your God will bless you in the land that you are entering to possess. [17]But if your heart turns away and you do not hear, but are led astray to bow down to other gods and serve them, [18]I declare to you today that you shall perish; you shall not live long in the land that you are crossing the Jordan to enter and possess. [19]I call heaven and earth to witness against you today that I have set before you life and death, blessings and curses. Choose life so that you and your

---

29. In his 1522 sermon on Christmas Day Luther writes, "There is no word in the New Testament that does not look back to the Old, in which it was proclaimed before. The new testament is nothing more than a revelation of the Old; just as when someone first had a sealed letter and then opened it. In like manner the Old Testament is a testamentary letter of Christ, which he opened after his death and had read and proclaimed everywhere through his gospel." *Sermon on Christmas Day on John 1:1ff., Church Postil*, 1522, WA10 I,1, 181:2 ff.

descendants may live, [20]loving the Lord your God, obeying him, and holding fast to him; for that means life to you and length of days, so that you may live in the land that the Lord swore to give to your ancestors, to Abraham, to Isaac, and to Jacob.

In the season of light it is paired with Matt. 5:21-37 where, in the Sermon on the Mount, Jesus is tightening the noose around our necks for our flagrant disobedience of the commandments, "You heard it said of old... but I say to you"; and in the Season of the Spirit where it is paired with Lk. 14:25-33, a word on the totality of discipleship is given, "Whoever of you does not renounce all that he has, cannot be my disciple."

So here it is, as plain as the day, "Choose life," the text declares in Deuteronomy, "Choose life." "If you obey the commandments ... then you shall live." It doesn't get any more conditional than that, does it? A propositional exegesis/presentation of this text would call the hearer to make a decision, to choose life. Your future is in your hands. It's there, your choice, as plain as the day. Read only the surface, and that's exactly what you'll find, and however you define life — personally or communally, you can call the assembly to a decision that leads to some action, some "application." But if you listen for the thickness of Scripture's meaning, the layering of the promises of the God who saves, there is far more to be heard. Ask who is doing the speaking, and who is doing the listening? Then think about the children of Israel and the bad habit they couldn't seem to break. It took many forms, but it was the same habit. Sometimes it looked like a golden calf. Sometimes it tasted like the stew-pots of the Egyptians. Sometimes it felt like the warm flesh of a prostitute. Israel had a very bad habit: They ran after any false gods they could find, and when there weren't any to be easily found, they made up a few of their own. They could run away from God and towards their own destruction with as much speed as any gentile, ignoring whom God had called them to be and how he had called them to live.

In this passage of Deuteronomy, Moses is preaching the law (TORAH) to them at an annual service of the renewal of the covenant. Moses preaches the law, so that they don't have a leg to stand on. Moses preaches the law, so that they will live as a faithful community. Moses preaches the law, so that anytime they try to be God, and lord their power and influence over another, they will be exposed for the frauds that they are. Moses preaches the law (TORAH), so that the grace of being called into God's covenant would be lived out in joy. For at the heart of obedience is a joy that is rooted in the trust that God indeed rules the universe in love, in mercy, in goodness. Hear, O Israel, the Lord our God, the Lord is One — and this One can be trusted. Can you hear him, calling you to love him with all your heart, and with all your soul, and with all your might? *Shema Yisrael.* Is this not also gospel, to think that we could live in such joy?

Every time Israel is called to repent so that she may live — for who can live when running after false gods; every time Israel is called to turn — the word is near you on your lips and in your hearts; every time Israel is called to choose life inside the *ritual*, i.e., within the liturgical context of the renewal of the covenant—she is called into remembrance of what God has done, of what God is doing in her very midst, and of what God will do.[30] Choose life — listen — can you hear it, can you hear him? *Shema Yisrael Adonai Elohenu Adonai Ehad.* The *Shema* echoes in every word of Moses, because although he is voicing the words, God is the true preacher, and God's word will do what it says. He will be our God, fighting for us against every power that wants to put an end to his goodness. His promise to be our God, our only true God, and all the rest of his com-

---

30. "God and God alone discloses the path that leads to blessings and fullness of life. God and God alone secures the journey along this path towards its intended destiny. Each refrain in this covenant liturgy (speech, text, and song) reviews the journey by tracing the community's movement with God from past to present to future. In each refrain the liturgy leads the community to recall God's *past acts of faithfulness* (29:2-9; 31:1-6; 32:4-14), *the present reality* of their own limitations and failures (29:16-28; 31: 16-22, 27-29; 32:15-18), and the future *hope* that resides in God who is willing and able to sustain the relationship, despite their disobedience (30: 1-14; 31: 7-13 [cf.v. 23], 24-29; 32:36-43). In sum, the liturgy asserts that the journey of faith is directed and sustained by God with a relentless compassion that will not be thwarted." Samuel E. Balentine, *The Torah's Vision of Worship* (Minneapolis: Fortress Press, 1999), 204.

mandments reveal the shape of an obedient life, where his love is experienced in simple human acts (2nd table of the law), for human actions reveal the thoughts of our hearts. When the thoughts of our hearts are formed in his thoughts, when the thoughts of our hearts are for the sake of our neighbor, his goodness, his trustworthiness, his mercy abounds, and the human community becomes what he has always intended for it to be — a reflection of his divine life.

The liturgy of Israel's ancient covenant renewal reminded the people that life lived apart from God was disastrous. These people were his, no matter what. "You are mine," he says at the heart of the first commandment, and he keeps saying it to every generation struggling through a wilderness. His call to "choose life" is not one of decision on our part, but one of anamnesis/remembrance and renewal, based on his promise to be our God. We can then confess that we are bound for death, that we are bound in sin, and that every time we've had a choice we've chosen the darkness. There is not one of us here who doesn't know that until we confess our rebellion, our wretched unfaithfulness, our lack of trust in his commitment to us, we cannot live. Without his grace, without his life, we could not even take a breath. "Choose life," he says, and the battle lines are drawn, but not between God and his people, but between God and the one who has us bound in his venomous fangs, between God and the father of all lies himself. The battle lines are drawn between God and the one who has been hissing to us all along, coiling around our hearts, whispering to the children of Israel to trust in themselves, in their own knowledge, in their own independence. The lines have been drawn, the battleground is our hearts, and the victory of faith, when it comes, is his.

Choose life. This is no proposition. It is a war. Choose life. It is a battle cry in our defense because God knows that left on our own we never could, and we never will.[31] Choose life, he

---

31. "There is ... one important feature of the Moab covenant that distinguishes it from the mandates of Sinai. In its vision of the future, the Moab liturgy asserts that the chasm between human failure and divine expectation will be bridged by God. In the face of human frailty, God will act to sustain the covenant relation-

says, and then at the very center of time he speaks the One who is life into our midst: The bread of life; The way, the truth, and the life; The resurrection and the life; The One whose word does what it says, calling dead Lazarus to come out of his stinking tomb — and he does, the One whose word says, "Take and eat. This is my body given for you," and it is; the One who inclined his weary head to a filthy thief on a cross and promised, "Today you will be with me in paradise," and it was done.

God had seen Israel run from him time and time again, so in a mercy beyond all human understanding he at last became one of them, conceived by the power of the Holy Spirit and born of the Virgin Mary;[32] At last, one of them, one of us, who would not run away, but who would lead Israel into the life of faith, and freedom, and joy as he crushes that ugly serpent under his foot (Gen. 3:15).[33] He, himself, would lead them to the

---

ship: 'The LORD your God will circumcise your heart and the heart of your descendants, so that you will love the LORD your God with all your heart and with all our souls, in order that you may live' (Deuteronomy 30:6). This clear echo of the *Shema* (Deuteronomy 6:5) is a reminder that the liturgy at Moab is once again a summons to *love* God absolutely and to *live* with a fidelity to God that is consonant with God's intentions. But in view of the frailty of the human condition, the question that must be addressed in Moab is 'how?' How can a community so prone to failure ever attain the obedience that God requires? In response to this question, Moses envisions a 'new' covenant in which God will prepare the human heart to meet the divine expectations: God will 'circumcise the heart.' " Balentine, 205.

32. "Deuteronomy teaches that repentance is not only needed, but that turning again to God is a matter of life and death. Deuteronomy calls for a decision: "If you obey, blessings; if you disobey, curses and death." Faith needs always to be awakened. New fuel is continually needed to feed the furnace of faith. Faith can flicker and go out. The prophets sensed this was happening. Deuteronomy programs a solution. "Turn, repent, live." Israel did not. Israel died as an independent nation. The failure of the deuteronomic reform to rouse the people to repentance and to restore an obedient faith to Israel points to the only real solution: God himself must become a faithful Israelite who can show Israel the way back to God." Mark Hillmer, "Faith in the Old Testament: Pentateuch and the Prophets for Pentecost," in *Word & World*, volume XVIII, number 3 (Summer 1998), 323.

33. Luther's insight on Genesis 3:15 set the stage for this discourse: "These words are spoken for the sake of Adam and Eve that they may hear this judgment and be comforted by the realization that God is the enemy of that being which inflicted so severe a wound on man. Here grace and mercy begin to shine forth from the midst of the wrath which sin and disobedience aroused. Here in the midst of

cross, the place of victory, where the sin of the world is exposed and the power of death is put to death. Truly, it is the place which none of us would choose, but it is the glorious place from which he will live and reign, drawing all who hear his word and believe into his everlasting embrace.

For between the Cross and Emmaus, there is an event to which there were no human witnesses. In that tightly-sealed tomb, between Friday night and early Sunday morning, in the inner life of the Holy Trinity alone, sin, and death, and hell are overcome. We are brought into that Resurrection moment, as God, Father, Son, and Holy Spirit, fills our assemblies with his eternal life, so that we, like those who came to the tomb that glorious Sunday morning and found it empty, we, in word proclaimed and sacramental love out-poured, can receive his divine life in ours. Through the performative doxological eucharistic exegesis of his life, in law/gospel preaching that puts an end to death and leads us into his future, all of us (the whole gathered assembly) become preachers of the resurrection. No longer shouting for his crucifixion, but gathered in thanksgiving we now cry out in joy: "Christ has died; Christ is risen; Christ will come again." Amen.

---

most serious threats the Father reveals his heart; this is not a father who is so angry that he would turn out his son because of his sin, but one who points to a deliverance, indeed one who promises victory against the enemy that deceived and conquered human nature ..."*They hear themselves drawn up...in battle line against their condemned enemy, and this with the hope of help from the Son of God, the Seed of the woman.*" LW 1:189, 190 (italics mine).

Preaching Law and Gospel

J. Larry Yoder

Worship is the regular weekly setting for the structured interface between the Christian — especially the laity — and the "Law and Gospel" paradigm. My friend and colleague Dr. Schifrin is exploring "law and gospel in liturgy and hymns. My assignment is "Preaching Law and Gospel." Preaching is conveyance by audible words and, sometimes, visible pictures or gestures, perhaps, in some circumstances, with a copy to peruse and read *ex post facto*. But as to intent and occasion, preaching is oral conveyance — proclamation.

A bit about the content of my call: I am a full-time tenured college professor at Lenoir-Rhyne — having begun there as chaplain in January, 1977. I am also a more-than-only-part-time pastor at Grace Evangelical Lutheran Church, NALC, in Newton, NC. Prior to being at Lenoir-Rhyne I served at Christ Church, Pacific Beach in San Diego, St. Paul's in Durham, and now for the last 20 years at Grace. I am every week celebrating the eucharist and proclaiming law and gospel on Sunday mornings, and leading mid-week Vespers after choir practice on Wednesday evenings. I am a founding member of both the Society of the Holy Trinity and the Seven Marks Society. I acknowledge One Word of God in Jesus Christ.

Law and Gospel in Creation

In preaching Law and Gospel in the parish, one needs to specify among several dimensions of Law. "In the beginning God created the heavens and the earth. The earth was without form and void and darkness was upon the face of the deep; and the Spirit of God was moving over the face of the waters. And God said, 'Let there be light,' and there was light. And God saw that the light was good…" (Gen. 1:1-4a RSV). The Genesis accounts specifically state that God created the heavens and the earth, and everything that is in the universe.

St. John writes explicitly that "in the beginning was the Word, and the Word was with God and the Word was God.... And without Him was not anything made that was made" (Jn. 1:1, 3b RSV). And God said, and it was so. Thus the Word is the instrumentality of creation. And the Word became flesh and dwelt among us and we beheld his glory. Glory as of the only Son of the Father. Thus, long before humanity entered the scene, God the Creator — Father, Son, and Holy Spirit — spoke the universe into being.

The current discussion among physicists and cosmologists of a "multiverse" constituted by many universes, even thousands of universes, has physics and astronomy as its foundations. But the possibility of such a multiverse does not challenge the standing revelation resident in the Christian Scriptures of God the Creator.

Genesis notes that in the created order God pronounced as good everything that he had made. Not quite "Good News" as gospel yet, but before the fall there were only two commandments. The first was *via positiva* — the command to procreate: "Be fruitful and multiply, and fill the earth and subdue it; and have dominion over the fish of the sea and over the birds of the air and over every living thing that moves upon the earth" (Genesis 1:28). Also bestowed were plants and fruit and dominion over everything that creeps on the earth. And God declared these things to be good. If not specifically "good news," it was radically new ... and declared by God himself to be good.

The second commandment in creation is *via negativa*, as the second creation narrative proceeds, in the prohibition: "You may freely eat of every tree in the garden, but of the tree of the knowledge of good and evil you shall not eat, for in the day you eat of it you shall die" (Gen. 2:16-17).

Laws of Nature

And, there is "law of different sorts" resident in creation: "in the beginning, God created heaven and earth," both forces and matter…and laws of the universe. Long before humanity – the resident culmination of creation on earth — entered the scene … several billions of years. With the LORD, the ancients said, a day is as a thousand years and a thousand years as a day … I submit that the geological and cosmological records suggest that with the LORD a billion years may be as a day, and a day as a billion years.

And resident in the creation are the laws of nature … the law of gravity and the second law of thermodynamics, among many others. God — Father, Son, and Holy Spirit — *spoke the world into being. The Spirit of God brooded over the face of the deep.* He ordered the galaxies and the stars, the planets and the seasons, all according to laws, the laws of nature. The laws of nature inform the content of proclamation when dimensions of the created order inform the immediate subject matter.

Humanity, on our arrival, even in primitive state, learned to take into account what came to be known as the law of gravity, the changing of the seasons, the difference between animals that were capable of domestication and those only tolerated or exploited from the wild … the predators from the prey. You can't domesticate a rattlesnake, even by snuggling and petting generations in the same line across a thousand years, but across time and generations a wolf can become, as they say in Lincoln County, a dawg.

As to the more sophisticated laws, like the second law of thermodynamics, it has been in the modern era that discovery, articulation and technical utilization have been attained. Those laws are physical laws of the universe, some of which, no doubt, are yet to be discovered.

The Law Written upon the Heart – Natural Law

There is also natural law, the law written upon the heart. St. Paul famously declares in Romans, the second chapter: "When the Gentiles, who do not have the law do by nature what the law requires, they are a law to themselves, even though they do not have the law. They show that what the law requires is written on their hearts, while their conscience also bears witness and their conflicting thoughts accuse or perhaps excuse them on that day when, according to my gospel, God judges the secrets of men by Christ Jesus" (St. Paul in Rom. 2: 14-16).

St. Paul is here giving reference to both Aristotle and the Stoics, who argued that prior to "positive" or written human laws are laws embedded in the universe — written, as the Apostle states it, on the heart.

More than a few of the founding Fathers of this country were themselves in the camp of "natural law" advocates. *The Declaration of Independence* states that it has become necessary for the United States to assume "the separate and equal station to which the Laws of Nature and of Nature's God entitle them." "Laws of nature and nature's God" may reasonably be interpreted as referencing natural law, to which constitutions, nations, and individuals may reasonably cohere. The key here is that even the Deists among them gave the attribution of generation to God ... rather than human construction.

As to Luther and natural law, Thomas Pearson writes:

> If it is true that Luther freely adapts the natural law tradition for purposes of exhortation in practical and political matters, we should begin with an inspection of that tradition. So what does the natural law tradition, as it would have come down to Luther, look like? What are the specific claims of natural law as Luther would have encountered them? This tradition may be summarized in five brief statements.
>
> There exists a moral law, objective in character, universal in scope and application, absolute in its authority.
>
> This moral law is grounded in God's gracious act of creation, is revealed in the natural order of things, and reflects the divine goodness of God.
>
> This moral law may be expressed as a set of precepts that frame and guide all moral deliberation and action for human beings.

These precepts of the moral law are known to human beings through the exercise of natural reason, specifically through the instrument of conscience.

The natural law serves as the necessary and sufficient basis and standard for all human law, including all positive civil and international law.

The Law at Sinai – the Decalogue

The central event of the people of Israel is God's giving Law at Sinai ... which constituted the event and content of the Old Covenant. This event shaped Israel as Israel, and furnishes the central content of the Covenant of the Law (Ex. 20):

I am the LORD your God ...

You shall have no other gods.

You shall not take the name of the Lord your God in vain.

Remember the Sabbath day, to keep it holy.

Honor your father and mother.

You shall not kill.

You shall not commit adultery.

You shall not steal.

You shall not bear false witness.

You shall not covet you neighbor's house.

You shall not covet your neighbor's wife, nor his man servant, nor his maidservant, nor his ox, nor his ass, nor anything that is your neighbor's.

Martin Luther rightly included the commandments, with his explanations, in his *Small Catechism* of 1529. The Decalogue is the starting point for the content of God's law, as revealed and given.

It is, after all, the first commandment of the decalog that governs the rest. For that matter, the first commandment governs also the Great Commandment, as articulated by Jesus: "Thou shalt love the Lord thy God with all thy heart and with all thy soul and with all thy strength and with all thy mind. And thy neighbor as thyself" (Mk. 12:30-31). The first commandment drives also the New Commandment that Jesus gave to his disciples in the Upper Room, "that you love one another as I have loved you" (Jn. 13:34). Why? Because the authority to command is resident in the first commandment: I am the Lord your God. Because the Nazarene is the Word made flesh, God incarnate. "I am the Lord your God; you shall love one another as I have loved you."

Law and Gospel

The proclamation of the gospel — that the Word became flesh and dwelt among us, that he was crucified for our sins, that he was risen from the dead, and that for those who believe in him he promises eternal life in his name — all this presupposes the proclamation of the Law. This theological use of the law is to hold before us our utter helplessness, how far short we fall, even when we do our best, much less when we overtly disobey or attempt to rationalize our thoughts, words, and deeds.

> Matt. 5:17 – Jesus said, "Think not that I have come to abolish the law and the prophets; I have come not to abolish them but to fulfill them."
>
> Rom. 4:15 – For the law brings wrath, but where there is no law there is no transgression.
>
> Rom. 7:7 – "What then shall we say? That the law is sin? By no means. Yet if it had not been for the law, I should not have known sin."
>
> Rom. 3:19 -23 – 19 Now we know that whatever the law says it speaks to those who are under the law, so that every mouth may be stopped, and the whole world may be held accountable to God. 20 For no human being will be justified in his sight by works of the law, since through the law comes knowledge of sin. 21 But now the righteousness of God has been manifested apart from law, although the law and prophets bear witness to it, 22 the righteousness of God through faith in Jesus Christ for all who believe. For there is no distinction; 23 since all have sinned and fall short of the glory of God.

St. Paul asks in Gal. 3:19 – Why then the law? It was added (to the promise) because of transgressions, till the offspring should come to whom the promise had been made.

We are justified by grace, apart from works of law. We have all been taught the content of the law, and the authority behind it. The law is not a human construct. Our time is less characterized by the theological tyranny of absolutizing "salvation through obedience to the law of God" than by an addiction to Cheap Grace (cf., Bonhoeffer), an addiction at once both casual and passionate. It is the case that old-fashioned "legalism" (i.e.,on the path to "earning"one's salvation by the quality and quantity of "good works") still has its quarters in both security and practice. Either overtly (here and there) or covertly in several "expressions." The content of conduct conducive to merit has lower stakes or higher, and more or less sophistication in the reckoning. In some quarters (i.e., communions), one can pretty well figure where he stands (with God as well as with the church) by some external reckoning of his ledger of morality or works.

The opposite pole of this fallacious calculus disregards "works" because they are specious under any circumstance and might even scorn "deeds of love and mercy" as "tainted," at best ... or, worse, not worthy of mention. All that counts is "faith." This kind of *sola fides* excludes or ignores, or at least devalues, deeds of love and mercy, rather than nurtures and yields them. To recall the apostle: faith without works is dead.

Our time is rather more prominently plagued by current segments of humanity — and certain "progressive" expressions of the church — redefining both grace and law or gospel and law as to whatever is their preferred content... and to such an *extent* as to declare as "*not sin*" what God has plainly condemned as otherwise.

Among the less gentle forms of such an outrage are several species of "autonomianism" (I became acquainted with *autonomianism* in reading *Veritatis Splendor* in the early 1990s), which amounts to the solipsistic usurpation of antinomianism in the service of one's own prejudices. In other words, one constructs one's own content to the law ... I will declare what is "good" and what is "not." *Kyrie eleison.*

To put it in plain English: *Autonomianism* means "I make my own laws," or more likely, "I will decide what is good. *Solipsistic* means that reality and truth have their proper origins in my thinking, my own being. This kind of reasoning is what leads to me deciding what is good and what is not.

The heart of the gospel — the good news — is that God was in Christ, reconciling us to himself. Christ' resurrection becomes the promise of our resurrection ... to those who in faith receive his grace and believe on his name. The promise is resurrection to eternal life.

St. Paul cites Abraham as the prototypical man of faith. What does it mean of Abraham when it is written, for instance, that his faith "was reckoned to him as righteousness"? Well ... post Freudian, post-Jungian psychology, and contemporary moral and spiritual arrogance notwithstanding, one needs only to read again St. Paul on the matter: "the words, 'it was reckoned to him,' were written not for his sake alone, but for ours also. It will be reckoned to us who believe in him that raised from the dead Jesus our Lord, who was put to death for our trespasses and raised for our justification.... [We are] justified by faith, apart from works of law" (Rom. 4:23-25, 28 RSV).

Jesus Christ *is* the source, after all. That we should follow him — instead of holding on to those for whom the Past is all in all — and instead of embracing every theological wind that blows from those who "will not endure sound teaching having itching ears; but *wanting* to have their ears tickled ... will accumulate for themselves teachers in accordance with their own desires; and will turn away their ears from sound doctrine, and will wander into myths" (I Tim. 4:3-4, RSV) — that we should follow him is both our call and our command. Of hide-bound legalistic conservatives and autonomian innovators we have plenty — of both sorts. Whom we also have — or, rather, who *has us*, and embraces us in his love — is Jesus our Savior, in whom is our life and our salvation.

There are some who argue that to claim Jesus the Christ as Light of the World is only an illusion. (cf., Freud) One can quarrel with secular "philosophers" who reduce the living God to "shadowy and abstract principle." But these words are less likely to inform our people than are attitudes of self-imposed darkness clouded by over-sated material prosperity. Who needs the Light of the World when we have plenty of megawatts? For many, the phenomenon of guilt, whether genuinely deserved or ego-contrived, is not the force that the prophets thundered or Freud analyzed. Some see themselves guilty not of sin, but only of "mistakes," or even not guilty at all: "what I choose is what I choose." To that kind of darkness we proclaim the Light of the World, to repent and live in God's grace.

To those whose groping for grace knows darkness and desperately seeks light, the proclamation is welcome. It is not infantile. It is the maturity of all the saints in light. Those people who have walked in darkness, on them has light shined — both law and gospel.

There is much in our present circumstance that erodes or obscures what is ultimately important. What is ultimately important is our relationship with God, who himself has addressed and accomplished what we cannot do. He has brought us to himself, from our sin and estrangement. For the ones whose discipleship is primary in their lives, *living the Easter faith* becomes both challenge and joy. The celebration of the resurrection extends to every moment and event of our lives. We need not be merely giddy or naïve. We understand the gravity of our own sin, persistent as it is even in our baptism as new creatures. But we live in the confidence of God's love and blessing, no matter what comes ... living within the constraints of the Law, fed and led by the Gospel.

Take the season of Advent, for instance. Our task is different, our proclamation of "the One who is coming" is cast in a different milieu. Expectancy in the culture during the Advent season is only commercially generated, by new products fueled, by advertising hyped, by innovation boosted: what's new this year? What novelty can be got for the one who has everything? Where Mammon is lord of a consumer pantheon, messianic expectation is truncated, atrophied, even redefined.

Sophisticates scorn John the-one-baptizing with the most damaging reductionism: that his message was only time-bound, announcing a messiah of limited proportions, one avenue to God, from whom there are sundry revelations, to whom there are many avenues of legitimate approach. John's message is obscured by Mammon, trivialized by pluralism.

But is the announcement any the less thrilling, the anticipation any the less acute — for those who believe? I think not. More the brilliance of the jewel that it should be so obscured, so scorned. More precious, for the ones believing, the treasure so put down. Proclaim the more joyfully the coming of the Messiah. Announce the more surely the need for repentance for the forgiveness of sins. Tell the more powerfully the old, old story of Jesus and his love. Share wonder at the manger. Pray the more urgently for the coming of the Christ child into hearts who yearn for succor amidst material plenty and post-modern sophistication. Understand both law and gospel in the proclamation.

I speak to you as a pastor and one who cares for the sheep at Grace Evangelical Lutheran Church, in the body of Christ.

Everyone who is here this morning is, and doesn't need to be told it but we reaffirm it again every Sunday, "a sinner by nature, sinful and unclean, who has sinned against the Lord and against our fellow human beings by thought, word, and deed; by what we have done and by what we have left undone." We confess it every Sunday. Having heard, and having made that same confession myself every Sunday, I make bold on the basis of the pastoral office to announce to the congregation, and to myself, God's forgiveness:

> Almighty God, in his mercy, has given his Son to die for us and, for his sake, forgives us all our sins. As a called and ordained minister of the Church or Christ, and by his authority, I therefore declare to you the entire for-

giveness of all your sins, in the name of the Father, and of the Son, and of the Holy Spirit.

Other than the words of institution, "this is my body given for you, this is my blood shed for you" and the accompanying words in the Eucharistic prayer, I say no words any more austere. In fact I suspect that "I declare to you the entire forgiveness of all your sins" is, at least on the personal and existential level, the most difficult, the most terrifying, and the most blessed thing that I say. And I say it every Sunday. This is done in Christian love and by virtue of the office of ministry.

But in today's climate of celebrating tolerance and diversity, even *agapé*-love is more likely to be invoked as rationale for including into the fellowship of faith behaviors the Scriptures plainly forbid. It is a kind of "love ethic" that fails to take into account St. John's brilliant complement to St. Paul: "Whoever confesses that Jesus is the Son of God, God abides in him and he in God. So we know and believe the love God has for us. God is love, and he who abides in love abides in God, and God abides in him.... There is no fear in love, but perfect love casts out fear.... We love, because he first loved us. If any one says, 'I love God,' and hates his brother he is a liar; for he who does not love his brother whom he has seen, cannot love God whom he has not seen. And this commandment we have from him, that he who loves God should love his brother also. Everyone who believes that Jesus is the Christ is a child of God, and everyone who loves the parent loves the child. By this we know that we love the children of God, when we love God and obey his commandments. *For this is the love of God, that we keep his commandments.* And his commandments are not burdensome (I Jn. 4:15 – 5:3).

During one of the panel-discussion periods of an Aquinas/Luther Conference, "On the Unity of the Church," Dr. George Forell remarked, with no little passion, to the effect that the Lutheran Church has forgotten the law and we do not know Jesus. Forell went on to describe how we do not preach the law as well as the gospel. When you do not preach or understand the law, the gospel is eroded of its power. It becomes meaningless. It becomes candy and ice cream. And if it does, we do not know Jesus. The Age of Pluralism makes Jesus one among many possibilities for worship and devotion, for life and salvation.

But we know Jesus as the Christ, the Son of the Living God. We know Jesus as the Way, the Truth, and the Life. We preach the Law as well as the Gospel. We do know Jesus.

Gospel, yes ... and Law.

Law, yes ... and Gospel!

Made in the USA
Charleston, SC
20 May 2013